LESSONS

FROM THE

DOJO

101 Kick Butt Ways To Improve Your Life, Business & Relationships

Rob Anspach

LESSONS FROM THE DOJO

**101 Kick Butt Ways To Improve Your Life,
Business & Relationships**

LESSONS FROM THE DOJO

101 Kick Butt Ways To Improve Your Life, Business & Relationships

Published by Anspach Media
P.O. Box 2
Conestoga PA 17516

Copyright ©2015 Rob Anspach

All rights reserved. No part of this book may be reproduced or transmitted in any form or by any means without the permission from the publisher.

ISBN 10: 0989466329
ISBN 13: 978-0-9894663-2-5

While they have made every effort to verify the information provided in this publication, neither the author(s) nor the publisher assumes any responsibility for errors in, omissions from or different interpretation of the subject matter.

The information herein may be subject to varying laws and practices in different areas, states and countries. The reader assumes all responsibility for use of the information.

Dedicated

To all those who are constantly seeking knowledge, improvement and happiness in their lives.

To my beautiful wife, Kim, who has been my rock for more than 26 years and has blessed me with 6 wonderful children.

And to Grand Master Roger Bradley who graciously gives of himself so his students get more from his instruction.

CONTENTS

INTRODUCTION

"A dojo is not just a studio, not just for fighting. It's the development of better human beings." - Fumio Demura

In March 2014, six months prior to my 3rd book being released, I set into motion the premise of this book. At the time, it started out strictly as a Facebook group page called, The Business Dojo. My intentions were to teach the art and discipline to those entrepreneurs who wanted more out of life, their business and their relationships.

The group page quickly grew and within a year there was over 1000 members. It was about that time when a friend asked me, "what's the purpose for the Business Dojo, I mean besides being kick-butt motivational and all?" I was about to say, "what else is there?" But, I knew what this friend really meant. How can it help more people and what purpose does it truly perform?

A few weeks went by and as I was watching my sons participate in their weekly martial arts practice...it hit me. Quite literally!

Things I was sharing all along on the Business Dojo could be turned into lessons that anyone regardless of background could benefit from. And so... Lessons From The Dojo was born.

There are 101 lessons broken down into stages (or belts like martial arts) that will help you navigate through life, business and your relationships. These lessons will motivate, educate, inspire, and maybe even frustrate you...embrace them...for they will guide you and develop you into a better human being.

And just like martial arts where the "Kata's" are designed to build upon past lessons, the lessons here in this book, build upon each other. Some compliment, some take a past lesson to the next level and some showcase a human element such as happiness and expand it.

So regardless of where your dojo is (the office, at home, in your car, on a plane, or a far off land) the lessons you experience through this book will help you improve your life and set you on a course that prepares you for a brighter, happier future.

Enjoy!

-Rob-

*If you find yourself with a couple of hours to spare every week why not check out the martial arts studio near you and enroll. The discipline you receive will help prepare you mentally, physically and yes, spiritually to life lessons. Plus, you'll develop a kinship with the students and teachers that will last a lifetime.

**From a relationship standpoint this book will help those struggling with divorce and failed relationships move past the bitterness and frustration to find ways to improve their outlook on life. Personally, I've never experienced divorce, but I've witnessed what friends and relatives have fought over and if this book can help just one person channel that pain into hope and prosperity then this book was a success. Being married has its challenges too. It takes faith, hope, love, patience and a lot of common sense...it's a struggle...but it's worth fighting for!

THE BEGINNER LESSONS

Your training awaits…

LESSON #1

Overnight Success Begins By Mastering The Basics. - Rae Brent

The basics…ugh! Who has time for that?

Well, if you are that type of person who wants instant gratification from reading a book, watching a training video or running an advertisement just once, then sadly you won't succeed at anything and this book won't do diddly-squat for you. Now, if you're the type of person who understands that success takes time and it's not always a walk in the park, then please continue reading. This book will be your guide to help you on your journey to master the basics.

Aren't "the basics" just common sense stuff anyway?

Well yes, and no.

True that most basic lessons are common sense, sadly, you'd be surprised at the many people who utterly live their lives without using common sense. The basics are also the stepping stones needed to get you to the next level. Each lesson learned takes you higher in the process. In martial arts it's the graduation from one colored belt to the next. In business it's using those skills to move up the ladder. And, in life…it's the difference between being someone with no skills to a "fix it with a rubber band and walnut shell" MacGyver type.

The next 100 lessons are those stepping stones that will help you master life, business and relationships, what you do with them is up to you.

I will tell you that it's not an overnight thing and will require your discipline, action and hard work to make it all come together…oh, but it will be so worth it.

LESSON #2

When You Focus On Fear, You Will Create More Fear.

Fear is that one thing that holds most of us back from enjoying our true potential.

Sadly, it's that one thing we focus on to try to psych ourselves from failing. The more we think about why we fear something the more we fear it.

When the movie Jaws came out, people were so spooked about sharks that it kept them from enjoying the beach. Some were so terrified that they didn't even want to go into the deep end of their community swimming pool for fear the shark would get them.

I've seen business owners focus on "what if" scenarios that cause them to shift gears and never launch the product or service they wanted for fear it would sell too little, sell too much, maybe it would cause harm or that it would be made fun of on a public forum. Selling too much, too little and any of those things happening, which incidentally, never occurred because the product was never launched...all due in part from someone focusing on fear.

This is my fourth book that I've written in the last few years, to some they will never write their first book due to fear. The fear of rejection, of someone not liking your work, is so strong that it prevents people from sharing their story with the world.

Instead of focusing on fear, focus on the end result.

Focus on the people that are involved and how they will benefit. Focus on you and how much better you will feel accomplishing the goal.

Remember, what you focus on...expands!

LESSON #3

Old Ways Won't Open New Doors.

In 1999, I was elected as the President of a local community club. I was thrilled to be able to show these club members new ideas to help bring in additional revenue, increase membership and ideally help more people in the community. Sadly, my ideas were dismissed as too radical and they didn't want to deviate from the "tried and true" ways of doing things.

The club was so set in their old ways that they didn't want to try something new. They figured that since those ways worked in the past, then they must still work, they would double the efforts and hope for the best. For them, the old ways of doing things became the very reason new opportunities were passing them by.

By picking up this book, by reading every chapter, by taking action and implementing new ideas into your life, you are opening up doors that weren't available to your past way of thinking. New opportunities, brighter horizons, happier relationships...the list goes on.

It's been almost a decade now and some entrepreneurs have yet to embrace social media. Yeah, I know unbelievable right?

It's the same principal; these entrepreneurs are stuck in their ways overlooking the very doorway that could help them build trust with their fans, friends and followers and eventually make additional sales.

The key is to be open-minded to new ways of thinking that will give you the opportunity to grow, to succeed and to teach others so the old ways don't prevent others from being stuck.

New ways! New opportunities!

LESSON #4

How Not To Be Successful...
Try Something Once, Say It Doesn't
Work And Never Do It Again.

Imagine if George Lucas stopped making movies after THX 1138, or Bill Gates thought coding software out of his garage 30 plus years ago was too hard and stopped.

Society would never have gotten the opportunity to experience Star Wars or grow up knowing the many versions of Microsoft Windows, or getting emails through Outlook, or playing Halo on an Xbox.

Tony Hawk, Michael Jordon, Thomas Edison, Henry Ford, Donald Trump are all examples of people who never gave up. When something didn't work, they would try again, and again, and again. Not just a few times...thousands of tries later until what they were working on became routine.

Maybe entrepreneurial success doesn't mean much to you, how about having success in your relationships?

Dating is one of those aspects of life that some just don't have luck with. All dating really is, is just getting to know someone... listening to them, understanding them, giving them a reason to enjoy your company and building trust amongst each other. Yet, as simple as it sounds, many find it hard and confusing. They don't pick up the signals or miscommunicate how they feel. Then the frustration kicks in and they say dating doesn't work.

Mistakes are the greatest life lesson we can learn from. Ignoring the mistakes and giving up is not something I believe you will do.

So stop giving up.

LESSON #5

Start Where You Are. Use What You Have. Do What You Can.

Exactly!

We get stuck on the notion that we aren't where we need to be to get started. We formulate plans in our head, we tell co-workers about ideas we have, or our spouse on where we'd like to someday vacation but then we don't follow through because we don't know where to start.

For those who grew up in the 1980's, hopefully you'll remember the TV show MacGyver. When he found himself in a predicament, he would look around at what was available to him then use those things to his advantage. It wasn't always items that you or I might instinctively look for, but things that could act in a similar fashion to help MacGyver overcome his dilemma.

That's the way you need to think. Stop being "hung up" on technicalities. Oh, but I don't have the right tool, or the time isn't right, or I'm not in the right place at the right time.

The time is now! Use what's available to you! And, that my friend is your brain. It's the greatest resource you have! Hey, you might not have all the answers or have any idea of the outcome, but if you do what you can using what you have, you will start to see immediate results.

Yes, sometimes you need to think like MacGyver and look at what's in front of you then see how you can utilize what you have to move you forward, get you out of jam or improve your business or relationship. No duct tape required...just a little ingenuity on your part.

Start, use, do!

LESSON #6

One Of The Most Expensive Things You Can Do Is Pay Attention To The Wrong People.

This is one of the hardest lessons to learn but one that everyone needs to discover early on. The wrong people can set you back and cost you time, money and lots of frustration. Oh, you try to justify these people by their stature in the community or business arena.

Hey, I'm the first one to admit, I fell for the wrong people too. It's easy to do. You get caught up in the feeling that this person will be the one who helps you get to where you want to be. Unfortunately, what happens is this person just uses you to help themselves go higher in their position.

One of my first high profile celebrity type clients, who incidentally was someone that I really wanted to work for, turned out was more headache than they were worth. The advice they gave me was counter to my own personality, my principles and my very fabric of being.

Oh, but they had friends with money and nice fancy things. Yes, we can be easily sold on someone's prestige, but that doesn't translate to money in your pocket. What happens in most cases is the wrong people cost us money, waste our time and put us months or even years behind in our own achievements.

The right people will encourage you, stand by you and give you advice which will put money in your pocket, cut time off the learning curve and make your achievements more rewarding.

Oh, and the right people will turn your personality and principles into a profitable venture.

WHITE BELT

White signifies a birth, or beginning, of a seed. A white belt student is a beginner searching for knowledge of the Art. The white belt is the beginning of life's cycle, and represents the seed as it lies beneath the snow in the winter.

LESSON #7

You Are Here To Do Great Things.

You have to believe that! YOU! That's right, YOU! There is no other person on this planet that has the same uniqueness as you. Imagine that, seven billion people on this green earth and YOU are the one that can make it all happen.

Sadly, you keep saying to yourself, "I'm nothing special, there are far better people than me!" That my friend is self-deprecating and will cause you to stay wallowing in the muck being sad for yourself forever. Stop it!

The very first time I had to speak before an audience I choked. It was horrible. I couldn't even remember my name. There I was behind a podium trying to give a speech to about 50 people about social media. I closed my eyes for second, took a deep breath and said to myself, "You are here to do great things!"

I apologized to the audience, pulled out my cheat sheet notes and read my speech. I know terrible right? But it was that speech that landed some of my first clients. They didn't care if I messed up, they cared if I knew my material and it sounded good to them.

Now regardless of where I am or what talk I am giving, I always repeat those same words, "You are here to do great things!" And, funny thing is, I rarely prepare for my talks, I speak from the heart, share stories and just entertain the crowd.

Regardless of your ability, or your position at work or your stature in life, remember you are unique and can accomplish great things you just have to remind yourself that nothing is impossible.

"You are here to do great things!"

Never forget that!

LESSON #8

Forget All The Reasons It Won't Work And Believe In The One Reason It Will.

You have an idea that you know in your heart will work and time after time you hear from friends, neighbors and even family "are you crazy?" Everybody that you know seems to be against you, criticizing or making some judgement call on what you know to be an awesome idea. Sound familiar?

Heck, Walt Disney was told not to build Disneyland, that it wouldn't work and that it would cost too much and be a complete failure. But as we know Walt pursued his dreams and hired people that could bring his vision to life. He believed it would work and it did. Millions of people every year come far and wide to enjoy the parks that Walt Disney's vision built.

Nowadays the notion of marriage or simply moving in together is one that friends might scoff at, they will tell you the statistics on marriage or how living together is such a killjoy. And, yet, contrary to the naysayers you look past all the reasons that the relationship won't work and chase after the reason that it will work.

It's not always easy. Taking a stand against what the majority is saying and deciding that they are wrong is not for the faint of heart. Some do get talked out of ideas, aspirations, dreams and goals simply due to peer pressure.

Believe in yourself, believe that your ideas (dreams, goals and aspirations) will succeed despite what others think or say.

Take action!

Make it happen.

LESSON #9

Compliment People. Magnify Their Strengths Not Their Weaknesses.

Insulting people is easy to do and it may make you feel superior in some way. Yet, it's fleeting and doesn't really do anything but make someone sad.

When you take the time to compliment someone you are magnifying their strengths, showing them that you care, that you appreciate the effort they are putting forth and giving them a reason to keep going.

Have you ever heard the expression..."the beatings will continue until moral improves"?

Well, demoralizing someone in hopes they will eventually learn doesn't really work. Yelling, screaming, using harsh words to describe someone are all ways to bring someone down, to attack their character.

Show people you care, give them a reason to believe in themselves, pat them on the back and tell them how much you appreciate what they are doing.

By complimenting people you will experience a tendency to live a happier life free from the stress and frustration of anger and frustration. Yep, being happy is a recurring theme throughout this book, as you will soon find out.

As you magnify others strengths, so shall your strengths be magnified...and people will compliment you. And guess what, the more compliments you receive the harder you will work to achieve your goals.

Bam!

LESSON #10

Be As Happy As Possible!
- Samantha Anspach

Sounds simple, right?

My daughter sent me this quote a year ago to remind me that being happy is all in my control. That's right! And, frankly it is that simple.

We allow outside forces such as the media, the Internet, Facebook, Twitter, friends, neighbors and even total strangers to effect our happiness. It's that empathy and apathy that plays tricks on our mind and keeps us in a state of constant upheaval.

We walk around with a chip on our shoulder, drive with road rage or allow what we see on the news to make us angry.

How is that being happy?

As the great Jedi Master Yoda once shared..."Fear is the path to the dark side. Fear leads to anger. Anger leads to hate. Hate leads to suffering." None of that sounds like happy to me does it?

When you are happy people treat you different, they want to be close to you and be your friend. But when you're not happy, well, that's a major turn off and it just repels people.

Before my daughter was even born, a person asked my wife why I never smiled. I never really noticed I didn't, but others did and they just assumed I was unapproachable.

So if you want people to approach you, to speak to you, to bond with you, to trust you... it all starts with being as happy as possible!

Yep, be happy!

LESSON #11

Kindness Is Not An Act...
It's A Lifestyle.

Damn skippy! Showing kindness to others is a life lesson that most don't realize is so paramount to our own humanity. Being kind to others goes beyond "random acts" and shows our true character.

As I was writing this book I came across future dates on the calendar and I noticed that in the United States during what looks like Valentines week is also "Random Acts of Kindness" week.

Really? Seriously? So basically one week a year which coincides with being loving to others we should be kind as well. Oh, my gosh!

Being kind starts with acknowledging someone, saying "hi", shaking their hand, then offering them your time to help them in whatever they need. Maybe they just need a friend to talk to, or a ride somewhere or maybe some food to eat.

Why don't more people live the lifestyle of being kind?

I think they worry if their friends see them, what will they say?

Or they are in such a hurry, that the very thought of being kind to someone will slow them down. Hah, we need to be slowed down and frankly if you are worried what your friends say about your kindness, you need new friends.

Kindness isn't random...but it is waiting for you.

It's always waiting.

You need to open your eyes to the people around you and show them that you are there for them, whenever they need it.

LESSON #12

Excuses Will Always Be There For You, Opportunity Won't. No More Excuses.

I'm too tired! I don't have the time! It's not worth the effort! I can't do that! I'm too fat! I don't have the money! That's impossible! It won't work! I'm not smart enough. What, me? No, no way!

Whatever your excuse I've heard them all. And, yet for every one of those excuses there is someone saying they can, or yes, or let's do it...they are the ones embracing the opportunity.

That's right, opportunity knocks but once on your door and if you are too afraid or just don't want to answer then guess what...opportunity goes to the next door. Someone will answer.

Stop the excuses...it's whats preventing you from living a better life, from having a relationship that's exciting everyday or from exceeding your goals.

Those excuses are your speed bumps that slow you down and make you second guess where you are going.

What if Steve Jobs said one day, "I don't think this will work, lets scrap the whole thing and stop our foolish computer building" Apple wouldn't exist as we know it today.

Excuses keep us safe in our own little comfort zone, but they also trap us and prevent us from seeing true opportunity. Excuses make us feel that we wont mess up, but what if the excuse you say to yourself is the exact thing that causes the mess up. Think about if you don't take the opportunity...you messed up and you will regret it for the rest of you life.

No more excuses!

23

Lesson #13

You Can't Stand Around Waiting To Be Asked To Dance - Amy Poehler

I remember my freshman year in high school I was what you would classify as a wall flower...I would stand by the sidelines waiting for someone to ask me to dance. I'd come home and my mom would ask, "How was the dance?". I would respond, "Okay, I guess". Then she would proceed to ask me who I danced with. When I said no one, she wondered why I went at all, seems like a waste of time and money if you aren't going to dance.

Yep, that's life for most people. They wait and wait and sometimes hope that someone will come into their life and ask them to participate, to dance, to be part of something...and they continue to wait.

How boring.

I stopped waiting and I started asking. And the dances got more enjoyable. This goes for life, business and relationships.

Years ago I interviewed Joe Sugarman the inventor of BluBlocker Sunglasses, and people would, after hearing this interview, question me on how I got Joe to do an interview with me. My answer... "I asked!"

If you stand around waiting for others you will miss out on wonderful things.

Had I never asked Joe to do that interview all those years ago, I would never have gotten to know him, learn from him and become his friend.

It takes courage to ask...but the rewards outweigh the risks every time!

LESSON #14

Just Because Some People Are Fueled By Drama Doesn't Mean You Need To Attend The Performance.

How many times have you been sucked into someones drama only to have it consume your life too?

It's awful.

Sadly, it happens more than you are probably aware.

I had a friend who was constantly texting her drama to her friends. She would screen shot the messages and gauge the reactions she got. Those who came to her side would be her friends of the moment, those who didn't would be chastised by the group.

Facebook seems to be the great drama instigator of choice nowadays and can lead to many unfriendings.

In life you decide who your friends are...not someone else.

When someone tries to pull you into their drama, you need to realize it's their drama, not yours.

Oh, and those so-called "reality" TV shows that you so love...guess what...they are designed with drama as the magnet to attract you to watch. You tune in week after week to see what happens next. Hah, just turn the program off, go read a book, take a hike in nature, clear your head and stop being the fuel that gives charge to someones batteries.

Just because some people are fueled by drama and seem to get excited by the commotion of it all, doesn't mean you need to be pulled into the attendance to see how it all plays out.

LESSON #15

One Of The Most Sincere Forms Of Respect Is Actually Listening To What Others Have To Say.

This is one I even have a tough time following...it's so difficult when we are constantly "plugged in". We take our cell phones every where, we check them, we answer them or send texts or check our status updates in restaurants, churches and even while in meetings.

Then instead of listening intently to what others are saying we talk over them. We say what we want to say never actually listening to what others are saying. Then we go back to what we were doing on our phones. UGH!

Put the phones away! Have respect for the one you are talking to. Enjoy their company. Listen to what they are saying. Let it sink in.

Listening is by far one of the best ways to improve your relationship with another regardless if at work or at home. Clients, colleagues, your spouse or even with a friend listening is the key to opening the doors to great conversation.

The next time you are out to eat, make it a point to leave your phones in the car.

Don't be distracted by outside forces.

Just listen to what the other has to say. By listening, you will gain their respect and actually understand the person better. Listen to their stories, learn about their pain and their joy, know what they stand for and why.

Be a friend...not a distraction.

Listen!

LESSON #16

There's Something In You
The World Needs.

When you're feeling down and out, broken or think it's the end of the line and you just want to end it...I want you to think about this lesson. Because, honestly, no matter what is going on in your life, the pain, the frustration, the anger or the sense you no longer belong...I want you to remember...there's something in YOU the world needs.

That's right, YOU!

Maybe you don't fully understand the power you have.

Or it hasn't been explained in a way that makes sense to you.

Whether it's your passion, your musical ability, your storytelling or take charge attitude...it's what makes you, you!

For me it's how I explain things to people in a way that makes sense, it's probably why I'm also great with social media and search engine optimization...I understand the dynamics of using words that educate, entertain and engage an audience.

If someone asked you what your super power is, what would you tell them?

It's what others see in you...and yet, you fail to see it in yourself. But, it's that something that others see in you that is your super power and that's why your friends like you so much for it.

Maybe it's your kindness, your sarcasm, your humor or possibly it's the way you tend to see the spiritual side of life...

...and that my friend is why the world needs you!

LESSON #17

When Smart Walks In You Pay It. When Dumb Walks In, You Don't Hire It, Even If It's Free!

Free is a powerful word, it's compelling and heck, just the sound of it and you know you don't have to pay a stinkin' cent for it.

But is it worth it?

The Internet has given us the ability to find practically anything, yet it doesn't teach us how to implement what we find. Right there is the difference between hiring smart or dumb.

Do you want someone who has the experience that can show you step by step how it all works so that you are making money (or some sort of progress) right out of the gate? Then you need smart! If you think you can scrape by and just try the free stuff in hopes that it works...well, good luck with that. That's how dumb thinks!

Hey, I've been there and done that...when I didn't money I tried the FREE avenue and boy, let me tell you, it took twice as long and three times as much money. Oh, and the learning curve killed me. It was horrible.

Had I known that it would take as long as it did and cost me what it had, I would have gladly just hired smart to begin with.

Oh, but it's FREE!

Shouldn't even be a concept when you are thinking of hiring a consultant to help you build the business of your dreams.

Hire smart every time, at whatever the cost...it will be cheaper in long run.

LESSON #18

You'll Never Become Who You Want To Be If You Keep Blaming Everyone Else For Who You Are Now.

I've run into so many people over the last year who think it's okay to blame others for the outcomes in their lives. These people harbor hate, remorse, anger and downright disgust for how they turned out.

They blame teachers, bosses, neighbors and even ex-spouses for things that could have been.

"It's not fair!", they convinced themselves, as if that helps them justify their situation.

You cannot correct your mistakes by pointing out the mistakes of others! But you must be big enough to admit when you make mistakes and be willing to correct them.

So what if someone hurt you in the past...it's the past..it's over!

Let it be!

Learn from it, accept it, use it...but don't be haunted by it.

Don't let the actions of someone in the past prevent you from achieving greatness in the future. Blaming others is what's holding you back and haunting from seeing the greater good in yourself.

Nick Vujicic was born with no legs and no arms, and you'd think this man would blame somebody...nope! He travels across the globe encouraging others to make the best of their lives and be grateful for what they do have.

So instead of blaming others, find a reason to inspire others and be grateful for their friendship.

LESSON #19

When You Believe In Yourself You Become Greater Than Any Obstacle And Equal To Any Challenge.

I want you to look in the mirror...look at your reflection!

Do you believe in the ability of the person you are looking at?

Don't say maybe, it's either YES or NO!

When I first started my cleaning business back in 1995 I had zero confidence and no matter how much I tried to convince someone that I was their best choice, no matter what I said didn't sound convincing.

It wasn't until I realized that I needed to believe in myself.

Yes, that moment that I started believing in me was when sales took off.

Oh, and it had nothing to do with lowering price...nope, my prices were 30% higher than my competition...it was the fact that I believed in my abilities and that was what convinced people to buy from me.

Doubt becomes the obstacle that hinders your growth and prevents you from overcoming challenges in your life. When you can look at yourself and see the person you want to be you can accomplish anything you put your mind to. It's up to you.

You have the power to "change your stars" and be more than you presently think you are capable of... but first, it starts with believing in YOU!

Your mindset dictates your outcome...believe in yourself!

LESSON #20

You Did Not Wake Up To Be Mediocre!

How about that! I bet no one has ever said that to you. Have they?

Well, it's true...you did not wake up to mediocre!

This is one of those lessons that may just have you scratching your head wondering what the heck you did wake up for anyway.

I mean seriously what are doing with your life? You seem to have a routine down, and to tell you the truth it's kind of boring. If I were to ask any of your friends what they thought of you...how many would label you as mediocre? How many would doubt your ability to be anything more than mediocre?

When you were a kid what did you want to me be when you grew up? I doubt it's anywhere close to what you are know, am I right?

Look, you have the potential to change the world.

What's holding you back? Fear? Money? Knowledge? Skills?

All those things are great to have and they certainly will add to your credibility...but, none of it is needed. Nope!

The only thing needed to escape being labeled mediocre is action.

Yes, action!

Taking action against your routine, changing the dynamic of your day and creating a new pattern that helps you move in a new direction.

No longer will you wake up living in a mediocre world...every day you take new action, and that action will help you conquer your fears, make more money, improve your skills and educate yourself so that one day you will conquer your dreams.

LESSON #21

Believe In Yourself And Never Give Up.

Believe in the goals and visions that set you for yourself.

In the introduction to this book, I talked about how I knew 25 years ago what my vision of myself was.. I could see myself on stage giving talks. I also mentioned that I hated being on stage and feared giving talks. So why have a vision of something that scared the living daylights out of me?

You see, I knew if I could conquer that fear of speaking then everything would be easy. I took speaking classes in college...barely passed the course. I even became President of a community organization just to force myself to speak in front of people. I think they were glad when my term was up.

It's never easy. But its so worth it when you finally realize you never gave up on yourself and you believed what would happen became a reality.

As I write this, my friend is battling cancer and instead of taking the "woe is me" attitude and giving up. He has embraced the fact that life is a game and in order to win, you must believe in yourself and never give up. In fact, he created a whole campaign of educating people using the hashtag #LifeWins.

Like I said, it's not easy. If it was, nobody would ever experience the joys of conquering their goals seeing their visions come to life...it would just happen.

No, we have to do it this way.

It's one of those life lessons.

Never give up, never surrender!

YELLOW BELT

Yellow signifies the first beams of sunlight which shines upon the seed giving it new strength with the beginning of new life. A yellow belt student is given his first ray of knowledge, opening his mind, from his instructors.

LESSON #22

Once You Learn To Quit
It Becomes A Habit - Vince Lombardi

I remember when I was young I would be interested in all types of sports, but I honestly wasn't that athletic. I joined wrestling because I thought it was cool, but quit after about 2 weeks because as it turned out it wasn't cool at all, it was friggin' hot, sweaty and stank of old socks. Oh, and getting your head slammed on a rubber mat was not my idea of fun.

Nope not for me.

Then I joined track thinking I could run, heck, I liked to run. After my first track meet I fell and scraped up my legs and hands, then I quit. After awhile of joining stuff and quitting, my dad said that I needed to stick it out and finish what I started. And just like Vince Lombardi said, once you learn to quit it becomes a habit.

For me and I'm sure millions of others, quitting became the easy way out. The more you do it the easier it is.

Quitting sports is one thing...but once the habit of quitting is ingrained in your mindset, you will quit jobs, organizations, churches, relationships and sometimes life itself.

Stick it out...give it your best shot...see how it all plays out, you may be surprised that you actually enjoy playing sports, or being at your job, and that relationship of yours might take on a whole new meaning and the message you hear at church might seem more inspiring.

Break the habit!

Stop quitting!

LESSON #23

Saying "You'll Try" Is Expressing "I'm Not Really Committed".

"Oh just try it", they say...as if the world will somehow be better if you try. But, that's exactly the point of you saying "I'll try" doesn't mean the world will take notice and say "holy shit man, you did it".

It doesn't work that way.

I remember as a kid I would say "I'll try" just to make others feel I was giving some half-ass attempt to play by their rules or participate in whatever they were doing. It never ended well and I, most of times, ended up getting in an argument with someone.

Funny thing, I see the same negative not really committed "I'll try" attitude in a lot of entrepreneurs, couples and even athletes. It's a close minded approach, maybe even a last ditch attempt to make something work.

They've already given up and the whole "I'll try" is their way of making the other person feel better, but the person "trying" isn't really committed so they don't put forth a real effort and they can say, "well, I tried, I told you it wasn't going to work."

Look, we all know what Yoda once said... "Do or do not, there is no try".

You either give 100% or give nothing. There is no in between.

Make a commitment to yourself and those around you that you will give 100% all the time.

Don't try...just do!

LESSON #24

Having A Good Attitude Matters.

"OH YEAH!", my buddy Doug Heiferman says that a lot! It's his catch phrase. It's also his way to remind himself that having a good attitude about everything truly helps in life.

Some would say "f-that" and blame the world on all their problems, as if the world was really out to get them. A crappy attitude doesn't get you anywhere in life, except making you a bitter, lonely person. Yeah, that's right…having a poor attitude will make you lonely as in no friends.

An attitude of gratitude (being thankful for what you have) will give people an idea of your character, they'll actually want to be around you and your positive attitude will be contagious.

A good attitude starts by getting rid of the negative energy that flows through you. I know, sounds hokey right? But, negative thinking (the thoughts you get from watching the news, listening to others complain, witnessing violence, etc) creates a negative attitude.

Yes, a good attitude matters. It's the difference between being called a winner or a loser. People will definitely think you are a winner when they see the good attitude you live by.

When hiring employees I always choose the person with a good attitude, even if they aren't the best qualified. A person with a good attitude will be easier to train and coincidentally will make me more money.

With a good attitude anything is possible.

Can I get an, "OH, YEAH!"

LESSON #25

Everything Happens For A Reason. Sometimes That Reason Is You Are Stupid And Make Bad Decisions.

Accept it! You became blinded by your own stupidity.

You blast out of the gate excited to try something but soon realize you're wearing blinders and have no clear direction where you're going.

It's clear even to others you are "flying by the seat of our pants" with no manual to help guide you. And that's when the bad decisions seem to multiply. Stubborn, stupid and just plain out of character, yep, been there, done that.

Then it hits you...maybe not right away...but eventually, that the mistakes you've been making will in fact be an incredible life lesson that hopefully you will learn from. A lesson that you share with others to help them benefit from you being stupid and making bad decisions.

Prison is the result of being stupid and making bad decisions, divorce can be too! Both seem like bad things, and yet, by learning from those stupid mistakes you made you can focus on using those as examples to help better your life upon leaving prison or starting a new relationship.

I had my share of stupid and frankly the mistakes I made cost me tons of money and years of hard work to correct.

The key is to learn from your mistakes so you don't act stupid in the future and make bad decisions that can't be fixed.

Think smart!

LESSON #26

Stop Saying "I Wish".
Start Saying "I Will".

"I wish I had that!" How many times have you said that to yourself? Everyday people wish for a better life, a more profitable business or a fantastic relationship and yet, that's all it is.

A wish!

We've been programmed from birth to think "wishes" are something magical and more we wish the more chance it will happen. Yet, those wishes become nothing more than pipe dreams.

Stop wishing! Stop saying "I wish".

If you really want those better things; the business that generates boat loads of money, a celebrity status life or a relationship that people envy...well, wishing ain't gonna do squat!

You have to retrain your brain and change your mindset.

Saying, "I will" tells your brain that it will happen and to get ready.

Yeah, it's a subconscious trick, but it helps turn those dreams of yours into reality. Saying, "I wish" is not commanding, it doesn't do anything for our motivation, there is no heart in it. Saying, "I will" immediately switches on those "take action" neurons in your brain and gets you to start formulating a solution.

"I will take my wife to Italy!", "I will have a sports car!", "I will have a bigger house!"

Stop wishing for your dreams to come true and "will" them to happen.

LESSON #27

Happiness Comes From Within And Not From The Outside.

Oh, yes we speak of happiness again!

Happiness is such an important element to the human psyche that without it we would live a life of despair and constant complaining. And, ain't nobody got time for that!

They say that money can't buy happiness...and to some extent that may be true. But there are a lot of people with money that try very hard every day to disprove that theory...they seem happy.

The abundance of money or lack of it, is an outside force and really has no impact on your happiness. That's right, it's the not the money itself...it's what money can be used for that triggers your emotions.

Happiness comes from a place of well being inside your heart and mind that doesn't change regardless of how much or little money you have.

Yep, it's a state of mind.

But have you ever noticed, people who live in happiness tend to have more friends, make more money and are presented with more opportunities? They are! It's true!

Your happiness is controlled by you. If you want to be happy, then don't allow outside elements to control how you think and feel.

It's that simple.

Oh, and happiness is not a fleeting feeling, it's a daily way of life that can have a deep impact on how others see you.

LESSON #28

Surround Yourself With People Who Have Dreams, Desires And Ambitions; They'll Help You Push For And Realize Your Own.

A support team! Yep, that's what you need! Yet, many try to do it alone.

It's hard to keep yourself accountable if you are the only one watching out for what you do. It's hard to keep yourself motivated to push forward or reach for the stars if you don't have someone there cheering you on.

Together Everyone Achieves More!

Yeah, that's what a team does, it surrounds you with a group of like-minded individuals who will help you achieve those dreams, desires and goals.

Exactly why most students who train in martial arts go to a dojo or why entrepreneurs join business building groups or why couples go on retreats together...they all want to be surrounded with people just like them who will inspire them to do more.

Associating with like-minded people who share your passion will help you achieve your dreams faster then going it alone.

Hey, I've been there...having the whole "I can do it on my own" attitude, only to realize it was costing me time, money and whole bunch of frustration.

Surround yourself with people like you who understand the value of dreams and desires, they will help you achieve your dreams.

LESSON #29

Always Trust Your First Gut Instinct. If You Genuinely Feel In Your Heart And Soul That Something Is Wrong, It Usually Is. Trust You Intuition.

Yep, it's that "Spidey" sense that tells you something just doesn't feel right. You know deep down that going along with the plan, accepting that particular client, dating that person or whatever the scenario doesn't feel right and in most cases won't end well. And yet, you do it anyway.

I've been there, many times. I knew in my gut that client would be a PITA (pain in the ass) and yet I disregarded my intuition and accepted them. And, every time these PITA's would prove my gut right.

Oh, but I would justify it by saying to myself, "Oh, its money to help pay bills", "They seem harmless", or even "I feel sad, he/she is going through tough times, lets help them out". Then without fail…reverse karma would step in and reward me with pain, frustration, aggravation, annoyance and thoughts of going "Rambo" on their butts.

Establish some mental guidelines that will keep you accountable to yourself. If a situation doesn't feel right, then walk away. No and's, if's or butt stompings about it.

Don't justify it!

When you become "in tune" with your gut, you will learn to stop bad opportunities in their tracks and focus on more of what feels right.

41

LESSON #30

Wake Up Every Single Day And Be Thankful You Are Blessed To Have The Gift Of Life.

Be thankful! It may sound trivial and some would just dismiss it as just that...but, it's quite simple...you are alive! And, that my friend is something to celebrate.

Yessiree Bob!

You have been given another chance to prove to the world how great you are. You have been blessed. Yep, the gift of life!

It's most powerful thing we have been granted and it's the most overlooked, under-appreciated aspect of our existence. In fact, when will the coffee be ready outranks our own perspective on being alive.

"Dude, I'm not alive until I've had my coffee!", oh I hear that a lot from men and women of all ages across this great planet. To which I reply, "You are alive regardless if coffee is consumed or not, be thankful". It's like listening to Ebenezer Scrooge say bah-humbug!

Really? Ugh! People, you have been given a gift...a new day! Go out and enjoy it! Be thankful! Some aren't so lucky and don't get the opportunity you've been handed.

Make the most of it.

Look at life differently. Be thankful for a new day. Be thankful for the life you have.

Wake up and appreciate all that there is...your work, your life, your business and your relationships.

LESSON #31

If You Want Change You Have To Be Willing To Be Uncomfortable.

Uncomfortable? What? Yes, uncomfortable!

If you want change you have to be willing to get down and dirty and do things that are out of the ordinary for your current mindset.

If you want to get thin, then the first step is to get off the coach and talk a walk. If you want to get six pack abs then you need to start doing exercises focused on your core and not just leg lifts. If you want to attract the perfect client then you need to stop dumpster diving for any person that moves.

Discomfort is needed to help propel you into something more, into someone more. It's something that most people will balk at and say, "ugh, that's too hard, I don't want to do that!" Or, "you mean I have to get dirty or sweaty or actually work to make it happen?"

Sad isn't it? Some people just want things handed to them, they stay comfortable living in their mediocre world waiting for others do to everything for them.

Nope!

If you want to achieve greatness in your business, your life and in your relationships then you need to make a commitment to yourself that being mediocre is not in your cards.

You need to be willing to get uncomfortable if you want change to occur.

It may not be pleasant at first, in fact it might be messy or strange or even risky...but that's what will help you be cleaner, more accepting and rewarding to others, to your clients and to your love ones.

LESSON #32

There Are So Many Out There Who Will Say "You Can't". What You've Got To Is Turn Around And Say "Watch Me"!

I've always been one of those "stubborn thick-headed S.O.B" entrepreneurs that when people say I can't do something, I immediately go out of my way to prove them wrong.

In 1998 about 3 years after I started my cleaning business I would advertise "no strings attached free carpet cleaning" just to get new customers...and my competition said to me "You can't do that". I would press them with "Why Not?" and they would just say "You can't". When I kept running the ads, they complained to the magazine that I was creating unfair advantages and they (my competition) would stop advertising if I continued. The magazine didn't want to lose them, so they insisted I changed my ads. I said I was going to keep running my free carpet cleaning ads even if I had to do it myself.

I removed my ad and created a direct mail piece that in the end was cheaper and attracted more clients. And those companies that complained about my marketing, well, let's just they watched as I surpassed them.

Why bow down and agree with what others are telling you if you know in your heart you can do it?

Prove it to them!

Prove to yourself that you are capable of doing things that others doubted you could do.

Tell the naysayers you're in control.

Say "Watch Me!" and keep going!

LESSON #33

The Distance Between Your Dreams And Success Is Action.

If all you do is dream about what could be, then the success you dream about will never happen. That's right! You see, when action is taken those dreams become reality and success a part of your life. Yeah, action!

Action is one of those things that doesn't take a lot to make a big difference. Nope! It can start as a tiny ripple that over time becomes a tidal wave. It starts very small and in the end becomes this enormous thing that has so much power and energy that it can literally change the landscape of the world.

Think of Facebook...it started out as a dream, that coupled with action become the biggest social media success story ever. And yes, it started out as a ripple barely registering then slowly grew. Today over 1 billion people enjoy being able to communicate in real time using the social network.

When Arnold Schwarzenegger was just 15 he dreamed of becoming a world renowned bodybuilder. He won the title of Mr. Universe at age 20 and went on to win the Mr Universe contest seven times over. Arnold turned his dreams into a Hollywood success story.

Success happens when you add action to your dreams. Without action, your dreams are just that...dreams. Create that ripple and watch as your dream becomes the tidal wave of your success. It's up to you!

Make it happen!

Take action!

Create your success.

LESSON #34

Your Value Does Not Decrease Based On Someone's Inability To See Your Worth.

Prior to being an author and speaker I owned a cleaning business, and what's ironic is my old customers still don't think of me as anymore than a cleaner. They couldn't imagine me as anything more than what I was...they couldn't see my real worth.

Sadly, that's that how a lot of people are perceived. And, it happens in life, business and even relationships.

It seems the real worth of a person is based on their current situation which is not how it should be.

That's their loss!

You my friend have the heart of a warrior and a set of principles that can't be unshaken.

You know that deep down you can accomplish great things, so why are you hanging around people who don't value you as you do?

The comedian Tim Allen served time in prison way before he became famous on the TV show "Home Improvement". But, because he had friends who saw his potential and knew his true worth, he was given opportunities to prove himself time and time again.

You can accomplish anything you set your mind to!

Your value is not determined by someone's inability to see your worth, your worth is determined by you and how convey your values on to someone else.

LESSON #35

Don't Let Where You've Been Get In The Way Of Where You Are Going.

In the previous lesson I mentioned prison. Being an ex-con is one of those labels that lives with you. I've never experienced it myself but I have friends that did and the stories are horrible. What's really terrible is that once people find out you were an inmate, no matter how nice a person you are...they don't want to have anything to do with you, in most cases.

Divorce can be that "get out of jail" card for many, but still has the same feeling of being chastised as being a former inmate.

That's the past...that's where you've been.

That's not future, that's not where you are going.

Yet, so many allow the past to get in the way of where they are going that they lose focus and they stop thinking about the future.

Learn from the past, don't wallow in it. You can't change what happened. But you can with some clear direction, understand how to use what you experienced in the past to make your future brighter.

Just because you went to prison or got a divorce or were hurt in an accident, that doesn't mean your future is over.

Nope, your future is waiting for you to rewrite it.

Where you've been and where you are going are two different things, treat them that way.

The future is waiting for you.

Go do great things.

LESSON #36

If You Are Always Trying To Be Normal You Will Never Know How Amazing You Can Be.

-Maya Angelou

Have you ever wanted to be part of the hip crowd, or the fun crowd or be like everyone else?

That was when you were trying to "fit in". Yep, and fitting in is just another word for normal.

You were trying so desperately to fit in and to be like others that you forgot how amazing you can be. You feel safe around normal people; safe from ridicule, safe from decision making, safe from risk...but being safe is not how you become amazing.

When you stop being normal and step out of the crowd you will discover that normal was boring and probably stifling too.

You see, as a "normal" you were afraid to spread your wings, to show off your talents or give others a taste of what you can do for fear they might make fun of you for being different.

Hah, be different!

It's okay to be normal for a little bit.

Think of it as your cocoon. You feel safe and secure. But eventually you will get urge to become the butterfly and flutter away. And, when that happens people will look at you funny, because they aren't used to you being that way.

Let people see the real you.

Be amazing.

GREEN BELT

Green signifies the growth of the seed as it sprouts from the earth reaching toward the sun and begins to grow into a plant. A green belt student learns to strengthen and refine his/her techniques.

LESSON #37

Everything You Ever Wanted Is Sitting On The Other Side Of Fear.

Fear is an illusion that your thoughts produce to keep you safe. Yep, an illusion. Your brain plays tricks on you to prevent you from taking risks, from doing things that might hurt you or from humiliating yourself in public.

Fear stands for... False Evidence Appearing Real!

Meet Dr. Guillermo Alvarez a gastric sleeve doctor in Piedras Negras, Mexico. Patients come to him to have weight loss surgery. But for many the fear of the actual surgery, the fear of not losing weight, the fear of traveling to a distant place, the fear of the unknown prevents more people from contacting him.

Surprisingly, when these patients finally overcome that fear and have the surgery they feel healthier, skinnier, more energetic and able to do things they couldn't do before. Ironically, those that fight the fear and go to Dr. Alvarez lose anywhere from 50-100 pounds. Some have even lost 150 pounds and the transformation is incredible.

Everything these patients wanted was on the other side of fear.

The same goes for you.

And, honestly if over 9000 people can get on a plane and fly to this doctor to have surgery, I think you can get over your fear and achieve greatness.

Fear is what's holding you back.

In your life, business and relationships...eliminate the fear and discover a whole new world.

LESSON #38

Life Is A Journey With Problems To Solve, Lessons To Learn, But Most Of All Experiences To Enjoy.

Amen to that!

Life is a journey, with plenty of problems, lessons and experiences. Yet, only a fraction of people who go through life will learn from those lessons or solve those problems or even enjoy the experiences. What a shame.

That's not you is it?

Oh, hell no, right?

The problems we face everyday whether in life, business or even our relationships help us become better people, well, if we take the time to understand what we did right or wrong. That's the beauty of life. We never know what's going to be handed to us, but like Clint Eastwood said in the movie "Heartbreak Ridge"... "you improvise, you overcome, you adapt".

It's not always easy. And, frankly it can be down right frustrating as heck. But, wow! Then it hits you...what an incredible life lesson.

It's those lessons, those problems and experiences that make for awesome stories to share with others to help them understand what they should do to overcome situations.

When I give talks I share my experiences, my joys, my pains, my lessons and yes, even my problems to help others. Hey, you'll experience your own, trust me...but make sure whether you are learning from others or catching what life throws at you...enjoy the journey because that's the lesson you can't ignore.

LESSON #39

Be More Awesome Than Last Year!

Yeppers, that's what its about it. Being awesome is a state of mind. No, it's not about being cocky it's about loving what you do, enjoying who you are with and living life to the fullest.

Awesome sounds like fun doesn't it.

And, to be more awesome than last year...well, that's what you need to do. You have to up your game. You have to be more mindful of others and how they perceive you.

Oh, but you're a wallflower and have zero clue how to be awesome...oh, what a shame!

Hah! Even wallflowers can be awesome.

Remember, it's a state of mind.

Just like everything in this book, it might seem hard at first, but with time, practice and repeatable action you will find being awesome is easier everyday...and year after year your awesomeness will be grow.

What? No, it's not some bullshit I just concocted to make you feel better...being awesome is something that anyone can achieve, yes even you!

Look, how you treat your friends, your spouse, your kids or even your clients tell a lot about a person and when they think you're awesome...that's your sign. Then all you have to do...is repeat that.

When people think you're awesome...then you're awesome!

That's how you become more awesome than last year.

LESSON #40

Learn Lessons From Your Dog: No Matter What Life Brings You, Kick Some Grass Over That Shit And Move On.

Yes, move on!

You can't change the past, what happened happened! So you lost an account, maybe filed bankruptcy or got a divorce...heck, maybe you even managed to gain the title of "most hated person on the Internet"...it stings and makes us feel like crap.

You can either accept it and move on or dwell on it, let it fester and wallow in the muck wondering why this horrible shit has happened to you. And, no it's not a frigging conspiracy.

Shit happens!

Back in 1998, during a thunderstorm, heavy rains penetrated into the flooring store I had at the time ruining all the displays, electronics, floors and even some client rugs we were cleaning.

Sure, I was mad. I felt like everything I worked for was gone. But a friend reminded me that "this too shall pass" and it did. It didn't matter how frustrated I was...in a few days, weeks, months or even years it wouldn't even matter.

Ironically, closing the flooring store and moving on was my best option as it freed up my days and allowed me to focus on the bigger picture.

Kicking grass over that "shit" put it all behind me and within 6 months I was making more money without the headaches of owning a flooring store.

LESSON #41

Never Give Up On A Dream Just Because Of The Time It Will Take To Accomplish It. The Time Will Pass Anyway.

In this instant gratification world it seems people don't want to devote time to grow a business, cultivate a relationship or design a dream. If it takes too long it's not worth it, seems to be the mantra lately.

Prior to my social media book *"Share: 27 Ways To Boost Your Social Media Experience, Build Trust and Attract Followers"* being launched in 2013, I would have clients calling me wondering why their posts to Facebook or Twitter were not getting likes, comments, shares or even sales. They didn't realize that social is all about the long term, and some would give up after 30 days because they didn't want to invest the time.

If you have a dream it shouldn't matter how long it takes to accomplish it...time is relative...and it will pass whether you want it to or not.

If you give up too early you will never know if your dream could be accomplished.

In most situations your dream takes just a few more steps, or a few more dedicated hours of hard work or some action that for some unknown reason you are not taking to fulfill it.

Relationships take time to build, businesses take time to grow, dreams take time to cultivate.

Never give up...keep going until your dream is a reality.

LESSON #42

Prior Planning Prevents Poor Performance!

Have you ever gone to a theatre and witnessed the performance of the play?

It's planned out, it's methodical, it's choreographed and rehearsed over and over. The cast knows every line, every step and every song to a "T". Yet imagine if someone who didn't practice was given a part at random, what do you think the results would be?

If you guessed poor, than you guessed right.

But guess what, that's how most entrepreneurs run their businesses...ACK...yep, a real train wreck ready to happen. *"Fake it til you make it"* only goes so far, practicing until you get good...is the only way it works.

In martial arts you just don't start with a black belt..nope, you start at the bottom, a no belt. You train, you plan, you practice and eventually that hard work pans out and you achieve black belt status.

When you plan, you take into consideration all the variables, all the things that could go right or wrong and you make adjustments so that when the performance happens you are prepared.

Prior planning helps create scenarios, plan "B's" if you will, that can help you in case things do go south for some reason.

Flying by the seat of your pants doesn't always work...but prior planning does help curtail the errors and puts you on a more solid course that prevents poor performance and helps make you a hero in the eyes of the audience.

LESSON #43

When People Treat You Like They Don't Care, Believe Them. They Don't.

Not every person cares about you. Not everyone has your back, so to speak. And sadly, when people treat you like they don't care, believe them.

The world is filled with people who for some unknown reason or another find it in their blackened hearts the need to bad-mouth others and cause ill-will.

One book I highly recommend you read, which incidentally I read about 20 years ago, is written by Dr Lillian Glass and it's called *"Toxic People: 10 Ways Of Dealing With People Who Make Your Life Miserable"*. Yes, it's all about dealing with and eliminating those people that are toxic to your business, your relationships and the very fabric of your being.

Get rid of them.

You don't need that negativity in your life.

Ever!

But, but, but, but....yeah, I heard it before. The excuses. They didn't really mean it. It was an accident. They said they won't do it again. Then they go and do the same things over again, and use the same excuses.

Some people just live for the drama, they have narcissistic personalities and feed on the misery they invite onto others.

Dump them. Get rid of them. Fire them. Unfriend them. Ignore them. Do what ever you need to do to disassociate with them.

Live your life free from the toxic behavior of others.

LESSON #44

No Matter How You Feel...
Get Up, Dress Up, Show Up
And Never Give Up.

Sure, there will be days when you feel down, crushed and ready to give up.

Don't!

Because no matter how you feel...it's within you to overcome those feelings.

So get your ass out of bed, wash up, get dressed then show up at least fifteen minutes early to wherever you have to be. You are not a quitter so giving up is not an option.

The excuses that people give today of why they can't show up for work, for their kids party, a date or even a client meeting are ridiculous at best. In most instances it's because they didn't give their work or the person they were seeing priority they only thought of themselves.

When you're unsure of your own direction in life, getting up, dressing up, showing up and never giving up are foreign concepts that have no real meaning. To some change is hard to accept. Crawling under the covers or escaping when things get bad seems to be the easy way out for some. Well, that's the wrong approach and frankly it shows you are not reliable.

No matter how hard life is, no matter how down in the dumps you feel you are, you look it straight on and say... "I can do this!"

But, it starts with you.

You have to get up, dress up, show up and never, ever, under any circumstances give up.

LESSON #45

The Fastest Way To A Sale Is... Just Ask For It.

Well, the fastest way to anything really is just ask for it. A sale, a raise, a date, an interview or perhaps even advice...it all happens when you just ask.

Yeah, it's common sense stuff.

A few months ago I interviewed Steve Sims, the founder of The Blue Fish. Steve created an executive luxury concierge service that serves quality life experiences to the elite of taste and mind. People loved the interview yet, the question that people would always asked me was, "How did you get Steve Sims to agree to an interview?" And, my response..."I asked!"

What if he would have said "NO"? Then what?

That's the simplicity of asking...you either receive a "Yes" or a "No".

Oh, but you have a problem with rejection don't you, so the whole asking part would never happen.

Get over it.

Because, I'm going to tell you right now...asking is the fastest way to get what you desire.

Sure, you will experience "No's", but you move on to the next person and you ask again. Hey, could I interview you? Would you care to dance? Will you marry me? May I buy you a cup of coffee?

Don't over think it...just ask!

It's that easy.

And, yes, you can do it.

LESSON #46

A Crisis Is Only A Crisis If You Allow It To Be Such.

I know so many people who get caught up in the "drama of the hour" that it paralyzes them from focusing properly. They seem to lose all common sense. They go into panic mode, over what?

Most times its about something trivial, something they couldn't control or an item that's misplaced.

Ninety nine percent of the drama that is deemed a crisis is nothing more than a minor speed bump slowing you down. Yet, it's turned into a massive mountain that causes you to have a meltdown.

A crisis is only a crisis if you allow it to be such.

Yep, it's another one of those mindset things. You can control it. Yes, you can. The key is not to allow the crisis of the moment to control you.

As I was writing this lesson a client called almost in tears, a situation occurred that was extremely emotional and he allowed it to be because he was physically worn down from work and travel and he thought he could handle it. He let a wee-bitty problem escalate to the point that it became a ticking time bomb.

Did you know that stress kills?

Yes, it can. When you allow a crisis to effect you, your stress levels increase. Too much stress and there goes the old ticker.

When you feel you might be losing control to the crisis take a deep breath, a step back, clear your head and just smile.

Then say to yourself "crisis averted".

LESSON #47

If They Don't Know You Personally, Don't Take It Personal.

I had just given a talk at a convention and as I left the conference room to mingle in the hallway where all the vendors were I turned around and bumped into the hotel manager. She looked at me, I apologized and she replied in a gruff voice, "who the hell are you?"

I quickly pointed to a sign where my picture was and said, "I'm that guy!" To which she replied, "and I'm supposed to be impressed why?"

She didn't know me personally, she hadn't experienced my talk and here I was about to "throw down" with this evidently stressed out underpaid non-friendly bulldog of a manager. I took her attitude as a personal attack against me.

That's when it dawned on me...

...there are people who are so caught up in their own bubble that they rarely care who they please or offend. They just want to get through the day.

We live in a great big world so chances of people not knowing you personally are extremely high.

Don't take it personal.

I myself would rather have a few quality friends that know me personally than hundreds or thousands of friends that really don't know any personal about me at all.

Quality of friends is better than quantity of friends.

LESSON #48

The Lower The Price, The More Hassles Involved.

How many times have you lowered your price in hopes of getting work only to have it backfire and cost you more time and effort?

I would venture to say…more than once!

It's downright frustrating isn't it?

And yet, I see the same entrepreneurs over and over again using low price as the attraction mechanism to try to bring in more clients.

UGH!

Hey, I've been there and done that…and it cost me.

And every time I broke my own rules and accepted a client that couldn't afford my price, by lowering the amount they would pay, it came back to bite me hard.

Low price is NOT a factor to win trust with anyone.

A higher price tells people that you are more experienced, well trained and know the true cost of doing business. And people that are willing to pay higher prices are more loyal, refer you to like-minded individuals and treat you with respect.

Goes back to credibility and authority.

Too many entrepreneurs get sucked into the notion they need to compete on price in order to attract clients.

Building trust should never be based on low price!

LESSON #49

We All Need A Reason To Believe.

Sometimes it's hard to hang on to a belief when nothing seems to be working in your life, your business or even your relationships.

Being an entrepreneur isn't always easy, neither is being a stay at home mom. Both endure long and thankless hours. Both need a reason to believe, that what they are doing is for the best.

Yes, a reason to believe.

Doubt, confusion, frustration, exasperation and trepidation seem to elevate our emotional struggles and make us question our very existence in the whole scheme of things.

We worry about our situation and if it's the best course of action, then we flip flop back and forth on what we are going to do.

When we don't have a reason to believe, the things we do in life don't have real meaning. So we "yo-yo" on decisions and make wild ass guesses. As the cycle of our uncertainty continues our situation seems to get bleaker.

Hope is in the belief.

When you start to believe in yourself, in others and in God (or whatever higher power you pray to) your life will take on a new meaning. You will be more aware, more excited, more energized and happier.

Having a reason to believe is what pushes you to be a better human being and excel in life, your business and your relationships.

Believe.

LESSON #50

Amazing People Do Not Just Happen.

What? You thought maybe they did? Hahaha.

Nope, it doesn't work that way. And they don't wake up one day and say, "Damn, I'm amazing" either.

Being amazing takes time. Just like mastering the basics, or getting a black belt or finding your perfect match...it's a culmination of learning, adapting and practicing to achieve your outcomes.

"Dude, you're amazing!" may be an expression of someone's excitement being around you.

What they don't see is the long years of practice, the grueling hours of sweat equity, the commitment or the non-stop learning required to pull off what amounted to 5 seconds of amazing time.

Yeah, if you want to be viewed as an amazing person then you need to work at it. It's that simple.

Although to some amazing is too much like work and takes too long to achieve so they settle for mediocre and they live their lives being ho-hum and boring. These people put in just enough effort to skirt by and maybe get noticed once in great while.

Look, if you want people to see you as amazing then you need to put in the time. If someone thinks you're amazing just because you're a good listener, then be the best listener you can be. If another thinks you are amazing because of your mad gaming skills then keep at it.

Whatever someone thinks you're amazing at, keep doing it...and more and more people will see you as amazing too.

LESSON #51

Make Everything As Simple As Possible, But No Simpler. -Albert Einstein

For twenty years I operated a cleaning business and it seemed, at least to me, that as the business grew it was becoming more complicated. So, I set into motion a plan to simplify my life.

It took time, energy and lots of patience. And yes, it actually forced me to get out of the cleaning business altogether. Now instead of a van full of cleaning equipment, hoses, chemicals and supplies, my job has been simplified to that of a computer and mobile phone.

Instead of being tied to my local market, I'm free to travel any where in the world. I eliminated the stress and strain of dealing with and maintaining costly equipment and I simplified my life.

Ironically, I consult cleaners who still think collecting equipment is something that is good for them to be doing, that it will help them get more business. Then they realize after not using that equipment for months or years that it was just a waste of money.

Make everything as simple as possible...in your life, your business and relationships.

Why complicate them with unnecessary "stuff" because you think it will help make things better? It rarely does.

Oh, and making yourself busy is not productive nor is it simple.

When we over complicate our lives we feel stressed and burned out...there is no reason for that!

Simple is better.

BLUE BELT

Blue signifies the blue sky as the plant continues to grow toward it. A blue belt student moves up higher in rank just as the plant grows taller. The light feeds the plant so it can continue to grow. The student is fed additional knowledge of the Art in order for his/her body and mind to continue to grow and develop.

LESSON #52

If You Don't Have Confidence, You Will Always Find A Way Not To Win. -Carl Lewis

That's right without confidence, you'll ability to win, to make a sale, to ask a person on a date or even write a book about your adventures will always fall short.

Let's go back to when you were a kid learning to ride a bicycle for the first time.

You might have started out with training wheels because you lacked the confidence to balance the bicycle while riding it. Then as you gained confidence in your abilities you those training wheels were removed.

This same analogy works for life, your business and your relationships too. As your confidence grows you can slowly remove the "training wheels" that have been guiding you.

Confidence in yourself is a powerful tool that will enable you to accomplish great things...lack of confidence, well, that will keep you losing out on everything you wish to win at.

Confidence is what helped Carl Lewis win 10 Olympic medals in sprinting and long jumping. He knew what he could do and was confident in those abilities and he proved that time and time again.

Lack of confidence and you will never trust your instincts, you'll second guess your abilities and you'll question your mindset...but hey, who wants more out of life anyway?

Well, you do!

Think about it...confidence equals a higher caliber quality of life.

If you want more wins in your life...you need confidence.

LESSON #53

Life Is Too Short To Argue And Fight With The Past. Count Your Blessings, Value Your Loved Ones And Move On With Your Head Held High.

I used to argue about everything. I suppose it gave me a sense that I knew everything or that I just wanted others to know that I knew everything.

Unfortunately, I didn't know everything and the people I was trying to convince that I knew stuff just saw me as a jerk.

Things that happened in the past became arguments in the present and it seemed no matter who tried to prove their point more, both parties would get stressed out . And sadly, what was being argued was trivial. Yep, a trivial subject was causing stress and tearing apart the relationship of many people.

Life is too short.

What really do you have to prove in an argument if it gets the other person mad at you?

These are the people you love, you friends, your family, your coworkers and your spouse. They are blessings not a target for unleashing a verbal barrage of sharpened words.

Why let your stress level get out of whack? Why argue over things that happened in the past that you absolutely can't do anything about now?

Move on.

Hold your head high and let the past be the past.

LESSON #54

Money Is The Byproduct Of Trust Creation. Without Trust People Have No Reason To Spend Their Hard Earned Dollars On You.

We sit behind our laptops sipping our lattes communicating with faceless customers in hopes to make enough money to cover our rent.

How is that creating TRUST?

Social media is awesome... but, its also limiting! We brag how many friends we have and yet when was the last time you picked up the phone and called one of the them? Not to sell them something...but to thank them for accepting your friendship?

NEVER...would probably be the answer.

How is that building TRUST?

You want people to trust you? Think old-school!

Use your manners! Be polite! Ask about them! Get to know them!

Every client has a story...discover it!

The more your client can trust you, the more they will want what you are selling regardless of price.

Building trust goes beyond business.

It works for relationships too.

LESSON #55

All Failed Relationships Hurt, But Losing Someone Who Doesn't Appreciate Or Respect You Is Actually A Gain Not A Loss.

Yes, you read that right! It's a gain not a loss. Yes, it hurts.

Tomorrow it will get better. And one day you will wake up and realize that person didn't appreciate or respect you.

I've been there. I had a friendship go south because they didn't appreciate the value I brought to the relationship. To them it was all about how they could benefit from my knowledge or how much they could show off my skills to their friends. The moment I removed myself from that situation is when they got upset and showed their true colors.

Oh, and let me tell you, the colors flew. It was ugly. And, it could have ended worse then it did. With relief, I gained my life back.

Yes, as painful as it was...I would have never realized how much of a gain I would receive by having them out of my life. It always looks so different when you are in that situation, then you snap and it's like WOW, that person is really not good for me.

Removing yourself from the environment of this other person allows you to "divorce" their bad habits and gives you an opportunity to experience life on your terms.

So although a failed relationship is painful, and you might think of it as a loss...it's actually a win for you.

Freedom is power!

Lesson #56

Don't Be Excellent,
Be Freaking Amazing!
- Solnishka Muse

You were told to be amazing in a past lesson remember?

Now it's time to take amazing to the next level! But I want you to understand that being freaking amazing is like having superpowers. And like Uncle Ben said to Peter Parker, "with great power comes great responsibility"...being freaking amazing is a powerful responsibility.

But here's the thing...that power, that responsibility is uniquely you. Yep, that power to be freaking amazing is in your hands.

Hah, no pressure right?

Ironically, those who forget the importance of being themselves tend to over copy what others are doing and sadly, they stop being amazing altogether.

The power to be freaking amazing comes about when people see the real you. Not you trying to be someone else, or model someone's business or copy someone's advertising...nope! It's about allowing YOU to be seen, heard and felt by those around you.

How you act around others; your sense of humor, your jovial attitude, fast thinking and love of life is all you. But when you try to be something you're not, your friends see that and unfortunately may decide to turn away.

It's about the experience others gain from you that makes you freaking amazing.

Keep it up.

LESSON #57

In Life, There Are Some People You're Going To Have To Lose In Order To Find Yourself.

Finding yourself is another phrase for achieving peace of mind and being one with your surroundings.

A stress free peaceful world.

There are going to be people that try to invade that bubble of harmony you created, you can either allow them in under your terms, allow them free reign or shut them out.

Well, from experience, I can tell you that if it's not under your terms than the other options are pointless. Get rid of those people.

Yeah, easier said than done right? You might not be able to completely eliminate these people from your life, but you can limit your exposure to them.

On social media it's easy to get rid of people you don't want associating with you anymore, you just unfriend or block them. Why should real life be any different? If they make you feel uncomfortable then they shouldn't be around you. Period. Stop talking to them. Lose them.

Over the years I've had to mentally say good riddance to friends, clients and yes even some relatives who were borderline whackadoo and were causing my stress level to exceed my tolerance.

Live your life by your terms and keep it stress free. Don't let weirdos in to wreck havoc on your mindset.

Set them free!

LESSON #58

Don't Forget That You're Human. It's Okay To Have A Meltdown. Just Don't Unpack And Live There. Cry It Out And Then Refocus On Where You Are Headed.

Shit happens!

That's life! And yes, it's okay to be angry, upset, frustrated, and you are allowed to cry and have a meltdown. But, what's not okay is living in that funk for a long time.

We are human, we have emotions. Use them!

Let it all out! Scream! Shout! Do what you have to do to get closure. Cry it out. Then refocus.

Everyone goes through pain and misery, it's life telling us that we are fragile and can be broken. Life is unexpected and unpredictable. It can't be controlled, no matter how much we want it to be.

Life's not fair, get used to it.

Now pick yourself up, dust yourself off and show the world that nothing can stop you.

It's up to you.

Stop rehashing everything that went wrong, or happened or why you are angry...the more you think about the negative, the more paralyzing it will make you.

Be positive, refocus that energy and get moving.

LESSON #59

If You Don't Know Your Own Worth And Value, Then Do Not Expect Someone Else To Calculate It For You.

This is a hard lesson for some people to comprehend...knowing your own worth.

You look around and you know in your heart and soul that you are destined for greater things. Minimum wage jobs...no way, no how, just forget about it...never going to happen.

But, how do you know your own worth and value when you don't even have a clue what that is and all your friends think you should be paid the same as them...piddly?

I see entrepreneurs copying each other's prices in hopes of gaining new business. Well, their prices are lower so I should be too is the mentality...thus, disregarding their own worth to copy someone who apparently doesn't know their worth either.

Do you think Donald Trump knows is own worth and value? Yes, he does and he's not afraid to tell people that fact. The Donald has written books, starred in a television series and owns properties all over the world...not only does he walk the walk, he talks the talk.

It's all about believing in yourself, trusting your gut and having confidence in your ability to make your prices, your stories, your writings mean something to someone where they feel you are the best person regardless of any objections.

You set your worth and value, not someone else.

Don't settle for what someone has labeled you. Believe!

Then take action!

LESSON #60

You're Excuse Is Invalid.

I don't care what is holding you back...money, time, experience, ability...whatever it is...it's just an excuse and frankly it's invalid.

You see, there is someone who is worse off then you who is making the most of life, their relationships and how they run their business. So, if they can do it...so can you!

So you're afraid? You don't trust your abilities? What is it? What's holding you back? Because that excuse you are using...is getting tiresome. And I really want to respond, "Whaaaa!"

Don't be a baby!

Suck it up buttercup!

Do you know what an "excuse" really is? It's an attempt to lessen the importance of something, to redirect the blame away from someone (in most cases yourself) or it's a way to explain or justify a fault.

Oh yeah...it's a fault alright! Yours!

You use those excuses as a crutch to keep yourself propped up...but they serve zero purpose other than to placate your desire to avoid something.

Stop being a pansy and put your big boy/girl pants on. Stop using excuses as means to avoid something. Like I said...there are others in far worse shape than you and still rocking it everyday.

Excuses are lies you tell yourself to justify your faults to others...stop it. Accept your faults and use them to shatter those lies.

No more excuses.

LESSON #61

When You Find People Who Not Only Tolerate Your Quirks But Celebrate Them With Glad Cries Of "Me Too!", Be Sure To Cherish Them Because Those Weirdos Are Your Tribe.

Welcome to my tribe!

Hey, in this dojo we cherish all weirdos. That's right, you're a weirdo...accept it. You're here to improve your life, figure out what you can do to get more out of your business and understand the relationship you're in to make it better. Yep, that's truly weird!

Your friends, the ones who accept you as you, the ones who don't point out all your faults and flaws are the ones who will stick with you through thick and thin. Finishing your sentences, picking up where you left off when you saw them last or defending your honor to another...true friends celebrate and protect each other always.

You never really thought about belonging to or even being the leader of a tribe did you?

Back to the weird thing. But hey, it is what it is. Accept it. You connect. That's great!

You spent a lifetime learning how to be you...and those who bond with you are the ones who share your same ideals, thoughts, feelings, music, movies and more...let them in and enjoy the world of you.

Celebrate your tribe, elevate your friends, cherish those weirdos!

LESSON #62

To Learn Who Rules Over You, Simply Find Out Who You Are Not Allowed To Criticize.
-Voltaire

Some people are afraid to criticize the US President for fear of "men in black" showing up at their door. Some are afraid to criticize what transpires at their job for fear of being fired. Others are afraid to speak up against their neighbors for fear of retribution.

Social media has become that "thing" that drives most people batty when it comes to posting. We sanitize our thoughts so as not to upset someone.

Recently I was asked not to comment on someone's post regarding a certain subject as they were trying to build a brand. Sadly, it wasn't their own brand. It was one of those multi level marketing products. They were so hyped on that product they failed to realize the damage it was doing to their own public image.

I posted anyway...then got unfriended. Oops!

Oh, well. It wasn't the first time I was asked to curtail my thoughts and it won't be the last. Yet, there are those who fear what another will say or do that they stay silent. That silence is their admission of who rules over them.

Don't be afraid to speak your mind.

You have a voice, use it.

Express those feelings and thoughts, show the other person that you aren't afraid of what might happen.

Stand up. Be heard.

LESSON #63

Everyone Comes With Baggage. Find Someone Who Loves You Enough To Help You Unpack.

We all have a past. And it comes with baggage. That baggage could be different things to different people.

Maybe you spent time in prison, or were involved with drugs or perhaps maybe you were a carny...it doesn't matter what your baggage is, that was the past.

The key to happiness is finding someone who doesn't care what you did in the past, isn't concerned with your baggage, they just want you to spend time with them, unconditionally.

I've heard people say, "she's got baggage" referring to her children when talking to another about why they don't think she's a candidate for dating. Really?

Wonder if they ever considered that, maybe, her husband ran off or simply was a abusive jerk to her and the kids...I say she had courage to raise those kids as a single mother.

Finding that right person who understands you, who helps you unpack that baggage you've been carry with you for years, who wants you to be whole again is the person who will help you deal with your struggles. They will love you no matter what you did.

Yep, everyone deserves someone who will help them unpack their baggage. To help them cope. To just be there for them.

You deserve that, right?

Yes, you do!

Let people help you. Let them help you unpack. Let them love you.

LESSON #64

Simplicity Is The Ultimate Sophistication. -Leonardo da Vinci

We talked about simplicity in another lesson, here we make simplicity sophisticated! Oh, yeah!

Learning to live a simple life is difficult, but not impossible. We have been programmed to need things, to want things to have things that frankly don't add value to our lives. We work hard to fill our lives with stuff that then requires more time and energy to maintain that stuff.

Doesn't sound sophisticated does it? Nope.

I see it in entrepreneurs all the time, buy this or that equipment to make the job easier. Next thing they know they have a room full of equipment that is never used, taking up valuable space and requiring costly maintenance even when not being used.

Nope, not simple...but very expensive.

One of the goals I set out for myself was simplifying my life...freeing myself of the wants and haves. Things don't impress me...people do. So instead of surrounding myself with things, products and equipment that doesn't really help me...I choose to surround myself with the right people who can help me do the best at whatever I'm shooting for at that moment.

Yes, but that equipment is cool. Okay maybe. But that doesn't mean it will simplify your life. Nor, does it mean it will make your business more money.

Don't fall for the "must have" trap.

Simplify and turn your life into the ultimate sophistication envy.

LESSON #65

You Know You Are Doing Something Right, When People You Don't Even Know Hate You.

Haters gonna hate!

Yeah, some people just find the oddest things to hold over someone, especially if they don't even know them. Celebrities, athletes, politicians, speakers and yes, even authors get a backlash from people that have some opinion on how these figures should act.

My friend, David Simone, a Las Vegas motivational speaker uses others "hate" to elevate and to motivate himself to push harder to achieve his goals and dreams.

Some people are downright bat-shit crazy jealous of others success or believe these people are undeserving of the fame and fortune they have attained.

If people think that of you...hah, know you have succeeded in doing something right.

Yep, pissing people off you don't know because you did something right, doesn't that just make you feel like you accomplished something. Hahahaha.

Look at Donald Trump, love him or hate him, he continues to make money, he continues to live a rich, fulfilled life...and frankly, he doesn't care what you think of him. I honestly believes he knows people hate him and he uses it, just like David, to motivate himself to keep making money.

Don't be distracted by the haters...use it to move up in the world.

LESSON #66

Each Morning, When You Open Your Eyes Think 3 Things... Thank You, Thank You, Thank You. Then, Set Out To Make The Best Of The Gift Of This Day That You Can.

Ugh, another day of the grind. I can't function without coffee. Can't I have just another five more minutes of sleep. For the love of Pete, shut that alarm off.

That's the typical morning of the majority of society. Burned out, stressed out, over-caffeinated, sleepless zombies who don't want to do the same things over and over again.

Well, when you open your eyes in the morning and give thanks and praise for what you have and the new opportunities that await you, your day will be more fulfilled and rewarding.

People, places and things will have a greater impact on your life when you have an attitude of gratitude.

Yep, that gratitude starts with a simple "Thank You".

Some aren't blessed with a new day...so be grateful you have been.

Use it.

Enjoy it.

Have fun with it.

Every new day gives you the opportunity to help another person, to right a wrong, to say "I'm sorry" or to simply be the best you can be...take advantage of them.

It all starts with saying, "Thank you, thank you, thank you!"

BROWN BELT

Brown represents the ripening of the seed, a maturing and harvesting process. A brown belt is an advanced student whose techniques are beginning to mature, and he/she is beginning to understand the fruits of his/her hard work as a beginner.

LESSON #67

The Will To Win, The Desire To Succeed, The Urge To Reach Your Full Potential... These Are The Keys That Will Unlock The Door To Personal Excellence. - Confucius

The will to win, the desire to succeed and the urge to reach your full potential...sounds all well and good saying it out loud or writing it on paper...doesn't it?

And yet, when you ask anyone who has succeeded in business, competed in an Olympic event or achieved celebrity status and you'll get the idea that those qualities of willing to win, desiring to succeed and reaching your full potential are the keys.

But what is personal excellence and how does it make you a better person?

Believing in yourself, believing you have the power, having the heart of lion, the courage to tackle any problem and the knowledge to keep learning are the exact things that make you into a better person, a person who lives life unlocking the doors to personal excellence.

What drives you?

Every person's will to win, desire to succeed and urge to reach their full potential is different.

It's the get out of your comfort zone, set goals, improve your skills and never take "no" for answer attitude that will keep you moving forward crushing it.

You have the keys...use them to unlock the door!

LESSON #68

Drama Doesn't Just Walk Into Your Life Out Of Nowhere; You Either Create It, Invite It Or Associate With People Who Bring It.

You're about ready to scream, your blood pressure is through the roof and that vein in your neck is thumping so hard you can't wait to high five someone in the face with a steel chair.

Oh yeah, drama!

But, honestly, that drama is something you can control.

Hey, you either create it, invite it or associate with people who bring it.

Yeppers, that drama just doesn't come out of nowhere, but you can tell it where to go. You have the power.

Ironically as I'm writing this lesson, the song "High School Never Ends" by Bowling for Soup starts playing and I think, wow, yep...drama is bit like high school. We want to know what others are doing, we talk about them, critique them, make fun of them, laugh at them and live and breathe their drama, which then becomes our drama.

Superficial bullshit that you don't need in your life. Get rid of it. Oh, but these are your friends! Yeah, okay, have a heart attack, or a brain aneurysm...just remember drama kills.

Drama is stress, and when you get rid of that stress you free yourself of the toxic behavior and give yourself freedom to live.

Tell drama to keep on walking...it's not welcome into your life.

LESSON #69

Sometimes You Can Over Think The Whole Situation And Miss Your Golden Opportunity. Say "YES or "NO" To The Situation And Stick To It.

Yes, no, maybe...um, I'm really not sure. Can I think about? Can you give me more time? I'm undecided. What if I make the wrong decision? Can I change my mind?

Sometimes, grasshopper, you can over think the whole situation and paralyze yourself into doing nothing.

And flip flopping back and forth is so exhausting. By the time you finally stop playing internal dialogue wars between your left and right brain halves you could have already gotten done the thing you've been debating about for the last hour...or heaven forbid days.

Stick to a simple "Yes" or "No" answer.

"Yes" you will do it!

Or, "No" you won't. It's that easy.

Stop worrying if you will make a mistake, just take action. What if the mistake is you trying to decide and you miss out on a date, or a profitable client or a chance to take a vacation in some exotic location. Yes or No...makes life so much easier.

But hey...if you want to stress yourself out and over think the situation that is your right...just not a feasible or practical one.

Keep it simple! Yes or No! No wishy-washy decisions.

Stop over thinking! Make a decision and stick to it!

LESSON #70

One Of The Simplest Ways To Stay Happy Is... Letting Go Of The Things That Make You Sad.

"Let it go...let it go...sad things never bothered me anyway!"

Hah, just be glad I'm not singing that song right now, then you'd really have something sad to think about.

Just like the previous lesson about over thinking we can also over worry...and that make us sad. It's okay to be sad for a while. But eventually you need to lift yourself up out of the funk and be happy.

What makes you happy?

Instead of thinking of the sad things why not think about the happy moments and use them to lift you up and motivate you.

I've seen so many people that focus one sad thing after another then they wonder why life is so hard or business is terrible or why their spouse no longer wants to be around them.

Look, nobody likes a "Debbie-Downer" so why be one.

Since I started this lesson with a song, I will end it with another...this one by Bobbie McFerrin from 1996, "Don't worry, be happy!"

In the song Mr. McFerrin says that in every life we have some trouble and when we worry we make it double, he's right you know.

The more you worry the sadder you become.

Let it go and be happy!

Rob Anspach

LESSON #71

If You Can Dream It, You Can Do It!
-Walt Disney

If you've ever visited any of the Disney Parks you'll understand the magic of how a dream can be implemented to benefit so many people. Yet, others didn't initially have that belief in Walt's dreams and turned down Walt time and time again.

In fact, Walt was turned down by over 300 banks before he found one that would help with financing.

Wow, that's a lot of rejections. Walt's dream was so powerful that he only needed to convince one person. Then it snowballed.

Now, Disney is one of the biggest entertainment companies in the world...not bad for a dream.

What's your dream?

How many times have you told someone your dream?

How many laughed at you?

How many believed in you?

Did they tell you to go ahead and do it?

For many the very notion of rejection is a powerful handicap that keeps them from ever achieving their dreams. They give up to soon.

You're not like that, right? I sense in you a desire to be more, to achieve more and to dream more. You have a never give up attitude and are always looking at the big picture.

The magic happens, when you can convince someone your dream is real and has potential. It only takes one person to believe in you.

LESSON #72

People Don't Always Need Advice. Sometimes All They Really Need Is A Hand To Hold, An Ear To Listen And A Heart To Understand Them.

One of my clients calls me his "Pennsylvania Dad" because I always take the time to listen. And, that means more to him than any advice I could give him.

I learned long ago that people don't necessarily need advice, they already know what they need to do. They just want comfort in knowing that someone is there for them...to hold their hand, to listen and to give them understanding.

The problem is that too many people aren't patient enough to listen, or to gently guide someone or give them their heart...they are too busy thinking far ahead in hopes they can fix the situation.

And instead of just "being there" for their friends, these "fix it" types are making matters worse.

When was the last time you just sat with someone and just listened?

How about holding their hand?

Or giving them an understanding heart?

The world is a busy place...you can slow it down just by taking a few minutes to listen to someone, to understand them and to hold on to them.

Zip your lips, open your heart...and just listen.

LESSON #73

God Didn't Give You The Strength To Get Back On Your Feet So That You Can Run Back To The Same Thing That Knocked You Down.

Abuse, mental anguish, physical pain...the list goes on, and yet, instead of removing yourself from the situation you go back for more. Seems counterproductive to me. Or, maybe you're just stubborn?

But what I do know is that the strength you are given isn't so you can continuously be knocked back down time and time again. You are given strength of mind and heart so that you can learn from the mistakes and move on.

Even in martial arts you learn that if you don't want to end up on the mat, you need to take steps to improve your stance and your blocking. Okay, maybe you're not in martial arts, but that doesn't mean you can't improve your stance or blocking to defend against being knocked down in life.

Haven't you had enough? Stop being knocked down!

If you're going to get back on your feet, then show the world you have the strength to do so. Stop running back to those things that knock you down.

God gave you the strength...show Him you know what to do with it.

Stop being stubborn!

Improve your stance and win back your life.

LESSON #74

Happy People Shine Brighter!
- Elizabeth McCormick

Oh my gosh, more happy people crap! Haha!

You'd better get used to it...happy people rule. Why?

Simple...they shine brighter.

Meet Elizabeth McCormick! She's a former U.S. Army Black Hawk helicopter pilot who now travels the globe sharing inspirational stories that entertain, educate and engage audiences of all sizes. And, she's always happy.

I first met Elizabeth in 2014 at the Lexicon Writers Conference in Denton, Texas where we were both giving talks. Elizabeth was forced to move her talk to the dining area and talk over people eating. She smiled the whole time. Her happiness gave power to her talk.

And, people hung on to every word listening to her stories of adversity, hope and flying the Black Hawk helicopter.

Yep, happy people shine brighter!

You have that power too. All you have to do is unleash your happy.

But how, you say? Well, having a positive mindset, carefree attitude and a willingness not to let things get you down is a start.

You don't have to be a former Black Hawk helicopter nor go off and gives talks around the globe...but you're happiness can shine bright for all to see. It's up to you.

Be the beacon for others to see, let your happiness shine bright!

LESSON #75

Always End The Day With A Positive Thought, No Matter How Hard Things Were. Tomorrow's A Fresh Opportunity To Make It Better.

The day was the absolute worst, everything that could go wrong did, and yet, you survived it.

Congratulations!

Can I fill you in on a little secret?

End the day with a positive thought. Yep, it's that simple. It doesn't matter how hard things were...having positive thoughts will help make tomorrow even better.

Hey, I've been there...I know how hard some days can be. It can truly suck. But that doesn't mean tomorrow will be that way, or that new opportunities won't happen because of how today turned out. But having a poor attitude doesn't help.

Even if you only had 5 minutes to enjoy a coffee or say "hi" to a coworker or read just one lesson of this book...that's a positive thought that you can use to make tomorrow's opportunities better.

Sounds easy, huh? Well, it takes a little practice. You're probably not used to ending the day with a positive thought. But, wow...when you start to do it...the days don't seem so bad and the opportunities seem more authentic and real.

It's up to you. You can end the day being miserable or end the day thinking back on all the positive stuff. It's your choice. But, when you end the day on a positive note, you're making tomorrow better.

LESSON #76

Life Doesn't Always Introduce You To People You Want To Meet. Sometimes, Life Puts You In Touch With People You Need To Meet To Help You, Hurt You, To Leave You, To Love You And To Gradually Strengthen You Into The Person You Were Meant To Become.

Don't shake your head and say it sounds like a bunch of hogwash, life doesn't work that way.

We might not always understand it, but life is there to always teach us a lesson.

There are people that I always wanted to meet, then I met them and thought, "wow, that was a waste". Hey, life has a sense of humor, accept it.

The best people that have helped me were people that I wasn't looking to meet. They just happened to be at the right place at the right time. Ironically, some of those people became long time friends. And, some have even been mentioned in this book.

Sadly, life also puts you in touch with people who will hurt you, but it's for a reason...and that reason is to strengthen you. The reason is not always evident right away and sometimes its downright painful. That's why they call it "tough love".

Help you, hurt you, love you or leave you...life turns you into the person you were meant to be become.

Accept it.

LESSON #77

If Your Clients Are Always The Problem, The Clients Aren't The Problem.

Businesses that are always complaining about how stupid a client is or what a PITA (pain in the ass) they are, tend to over look the fact that the reason the client is like that could be the way the business presents itself or how it treats customers.

Yep, most clients aren't the problem. We entrepreneurs would like to think so because it's easier to point the fingers at them. And, yes some can be legitimate PITA's. Some customer's attitudes are the byproduct of faulty customer appreciation.

That's right I said it.

The way clients react to you is the direct result of how you treat them. If you want clients to respect you, to value what you do and believe in your service then you have to give them a reason to do so.

This goes for friends as well. In most cases both your friends and clients are reacting to the crap you dish at them, then you get upset that they got mad at you. You are the problem not them. Apologize to them. Give them a reason to believe in you again.

Did you know that companies that use "live" operators instead of recorded robots are more likely to win over a client? It's true. Companies who automate their calls are not well liked. The last thing a frustrated client wants is to deal with a robot who doesn't understand them.

Stop pointing the fingers.

Look at how you treat clients.

If they are always the problem it's not the client, it's you.

LESSON #78

Don't Wait For The Perfect Moment, Take The Moment To Make It Perfect.

The time isn't right, I'm not ready, they're not ready, I'm not sure now, should I wait longer...sadly, I heard it all before. The same darn questions, the same excuses.

Too many people wait for "that" perfect moment, that it never happens. Or, it doesn't transpire the way it was supposed to.

Instead of waiting for that perfect moment, create your own.

That's right!

Why wait for the moment when you can take a moment and make it just right...just perfect.

It's not as hard as you think...and doesn't require as much time as you think either. In fact, the time required to wait for the perfect moment is in most cases longer than the time it takes to make the moment perfect.

Yeah...but sadly, its a concept that falls on deaf ears. Your mind is hung up on all the details and if one thing is out of place or seems to be funky in anyway, that perfect moment you were shooting for is lost.

Make every moment worth living for, make every second count and stop telling yourself that everything needs a schedule or a certain element to happen.

Be fluid in your decisions...allow ripples to happen.

Waiting for the perfect moment doesn't work. When you are flexible to the ebbs and flows of life every moment will be perfect.

LESSON #79

Actions Prove Who Someone Is… Words Just Prove Who They Want To Be. Actions Speak Louder Than Words.

Have you ever listened to someone say what they are planning on doing yet they never do it? Then there are others who just seem to get stuff done, and never once seek an audience.

Which one is better?

Well, as the lesson above states "Actions prove who someone is, words just prove who they want to be."

Yes, actions do speak louder than words.

Are you a "get shit done" type of person?

Or a "rah-rah planner"?

I would hope that you being someone that wants to constantly improve, see the wisdom in taking action. I would also hope that you truly understand how people perceive those actions you take.

Politicians are notorious for giving talks that are filled with fluffery to excite constituents into electing them. Then the excitement wears off and people are left wondering why they elected such a doofus to begin with.

Yeah, if you want people to think of you as a politician then by all means…no, scratch that…you don't want people thinking of you that way. Unless of course you are a politician, and you are seeking election. But here's the thing…if you really want people to think of you as a real "go getter" then action is required.

Prove who you are…show people you are a person of action.

LESSON #80

The Only Person Who Is Holding You Back Is You. No More Excuses, It's Time To Change. It's Time To Live Life At A Now Level.

Do you know the difference between being successful and just being mediocre?

It's that six letter word called "EXCUSE"!

A word that holds so many people back from achieving success in all they do. And yet, regardless of books like this, motivational videos or even guru-style seminars that make you feel all warm and fuzzy inside, the power to be more than you are resides in you.

That's right! You are the only one that can make the decision to move forward. Oh, but you're thinking you're not smart enough or strong enough or good looking enough or whatever excuse your brain is telling you. Look around Bub...there are plenty of dumb, weak and ugly people making money, finding the perfect spouse or becoming famous.

What would happen if you decided not to listen to that excuse your brain is telling you? Well I can tell what would happen if I listened to my excuses...for one you wouldn't be reading this book, or any of my books for that matter. They would have never been written.

If I can change so can you. And it's in that change of not accepting excuses where you will have a breakthrough and start living life. If someone invites you on a trip you can say, "Count me in" instead of "I dunno' sounds expensive"!

No more excuses!

Just do it!

LESSON #81

When I Look Back On My Life, I See Pain, Mistakes And Heartaches. When I Look In The Mirror, I See Strength, Learned Lessons And Pride In Myself.

Your reflection gives you a better idea of who you are than the mental picture you keep of yourself in that noggin of yours.

Don't believe me?

Go take a good long look at yourself in front of the mirror.

You might remember the pain, the mistakes and the heartaches that life dealt you, but in reality they were life lessons that gave you strength and pride in yourself.

How do I know?

Hey, just because I write books and help entrepreneurs across the globe doesn't mean I'm Superman. I'm human too. I have emotions. I've experienced pain, mistakes and heartache. In fact this book was delayed a month as I mourned the death of my grandson. He lived just 14 days, but he was the bravest warrior I ever met.

Once a day look at yourself in the mirror and see the person you've become. See the strength in what you've had to endure. Relive the lessons that you've had to learn. Hold your head high and have pride in who you've become.

You've earned it.

Break the mental image of yourself...look in the mirror and see the real you, the one who overcame challenges to become invincible.

BELT BLACK

Black signifies the darkness beyond the Sun. A black belt seeks new, more profound knowledge of the Art. As he/she begins to teach others, he/she plants new seeds and helps them grow and mature. His/her students, many whom will form roots deep into the Art, blossom and grow through the ranks in a never-ending process of self-growth, knowledge, and enlightenment.

LESSON #82

Balance Your Thoughts With Action. If You Spend Too Much Time Thinking, You'll Never Get It Done.

Over thinking prevents action from occurring and that very thought of doing something becomes the very thing that doesn't get done.

You play the "flip-flop" game and try to justify all the outcomes. In the meantime you could have gotten done the very thing you've been thinking of and moved on to the next thing.

Less thinking...more doing!

Balancing your thoughts with action will prevent you from spending too much time thinking...and amazingly you will find you actually get stuff done.

Wait, what? You're scared you'll mess up. Or perhaps what ever it is you're doing won't end well. Or maybe someone will laugh at you or criticize you. Yes, you might mess up and yes it might not end well and yes you might be made fun of...so what?

Suck it up!

Pull you big boy/girl pants up and show the world that their acceptance doesn't really matter.

Your decision is your decision.

Your thoughts are in balance with your actions and you are getting stuff done.

Don't over think!

Life becomes too complicated when people over think a situation, balance your thoughts and your actions become clearer.

LESSON #83

It's Not About Perfect. It's About Effort. And When You Implement That Effort Into Your Life Every Single Day, That's Where Transformation Happens. That's How Change Occurs. Keep Going. Remember Why You Started.

Don't get hung up on perfect.

Perfect is an illusion that will drive you crazy. Focus on the effort instead. Yeah, effort! Who'da thunk?

Just forget about perfect...it's all about effort. And, it's that effort that will have the greatest impact on your life and business, lead to amazing transformations and motivate you to keep going.

Oh, but you're still hung up on the whole perfect thing.

Do you think Apple or Microsoft are concerned with perfect? If you answered YES, you're wrong. Both companies operate on the premise that the majority of people will accept a product that isn't perfect.. Think about it. When you buy their products are the software programs up to date? Nope. These companies are constantly sending updates to fix a code, patch a flaw or add a new feature. They are far from perfect. And yet, they are two very profitable companies.

Relationships are the same way. Yet, when each person implements effort into that relationship every single day that's what keeps it going. Relationship die when no effort is put forth.

When you desire the greatest impact...it's all about the effort.

LESSON #84

Success Doesn't Happen To You, It Happens Because Of You.

"Oh, you're so lucky", I hear from so many people. They go on to praise the success that has happened to me, yet they fail to realize that my success didn't happen to me, it happened because of me.

It was the effort I put forth every single day that helped transform me into the success you see. Hah, yep, you caught it...success and effort go hand in hand.

For me, my success wasn't overnight it took time. In fact, as you probably guessed from this book, it took over 20 years to happen. I was not lucky as some say...luck would be if success actually happened overnight or even 30, 60, 90 or 365 days after I set out on my path.

True success is never about luck...it's about YOU.

It doesn't happen to you, it happens because of you.

Luck has nothing to do with it...ever!

If you're all about luck try playing the lottery. If you want success then you're going to have to be in it for the long haul.

Success happens when those efforts we talked about earlier continue to grow and those dreams and aspirations are accomplished.

Meeting random people is luck...forming long lasting relationship with those people is success.

Know the difference.

Your success is up to you...the more effort, the greater the success.

LESSON #85

A Change In Direction Does Not Mean You're Abandoning Your Path. Few Paths Are Wide, Straight Or Predictable.

Who would have thought 20 years after starting a carpet cleaning business in a small town most know for the Amish, I would be writing books and coaching companies all over the world? Certainly, none of my friends thought that. But that's my path!

I envisioned that path more than 25 years ago, in fact I could say with certainly the exact year I saw myself standing on a stage giving a speech to a crowd. Ironically, back then I hated standing on a stage in front of people and I certainly didn't like giving speeches. Owning a cleaning business helped me become a better entrepreneur, a story teller, a writer and a marketer.

I never abandoned my path, it's just that the path I was on was bit rockier than most and took me a few decades to navigate through. I think that's true for most people.

Most paths aren't straight and I guarantee you none are predictable...but that shouldn't stop you from taking the journey.

Your path could be leading you to own a business, travel the world, get married and have kids, write a book...or heck all of them, but whatever your path is, know this...it'll be filled with excitement that will make for great stories.

So even if you change direction, it's still your path.

Enjoy it.

One day you will look back and appreciate the path you were on.

LESSON #86

Wear Your Scars With Pride...
Because A Scarless Man Has Not Felt
The Hardship Of Life
Or The Feelings Of Pain.
And A Knight In Shining Armor Is A Man Who
Has Never Had His Metal Truly Tested.

We learn from our experiences...the good, the bad and the painful.

That's life!

It's those experiences that make us battle hardened. Seriously, who would you rather choose to help you, a person who has felt the hardship of pain or the person who has the shiny armor?

Lots of people are tricked by the "shiny object" syndrome and fall victim to being sold on "slickery" and fail to ask for substance. Their so-called "Knight in shining armor" is really just a "slick willy" con artist. Or someone so "green behind the ears" they don't understand how to use life's lessons to help another yet.

You can tell a lot about a person just by taking a few minutes to look at their face, how they carry themselves, the way they talk and the actions they take.

Be observant!

And your scars...you earned them. Use them to teach and inspire others about life's hardships. Once someone sees your dents and dings they will appreciate the real Knight you've become.

Accept the scars! Have your metal tested! Feel the pain! Show others your pride, share your story, give them a reason to trust you.

LESSON #87

When Your Past Calls Don't Answer It. It Has Nothing New To Say.

Ever hear the expression, "same shit, different day"?

Well, when your past calls...that's exactly what it is...nothing but trouble!

You left those people, problems, bad relationships, nutty clients, etc, etc in the past for a reason.

Why are you allowing that negative crap back into your life now?

Oh, but it will be so much better this time around, you keep saying to yourself while at the same time crossing your fingers in hope that what you are telling yourself will somehow placate your subconscious into going along. Hah, that never works.

Sadly, I see many people that for some reason or another think, "yeah, okay this time will be different, I just know it" and they invite the past into their lives with open arms. Then they watch as history repeats itself and causes turmoil in their life yet again.

They tell their friends that they felt completely blindsided and it happened without warning. Yeah, whatever.

As Forest Gump once said, "stupid is as stupid does."

The best thing you can do when your past rears it's ugly head is just say NO. It didn't work out then, it won't work out now.

And no matter how many times the past calls you, begs you, pleads with you or somehow convinces you to allow it back in your life...the answer should always be no.

The past is the past...leave it there.

LESSON #88

Don't Just Meet Your Goals… Destroy Them!

About 18 years ago I was listening to an interview by "Chicken Soup for The Soul" coauthor Mark Victor Hansen. During the interview he talked about writing down your goals. He suggested writing down at least 100 goals you wanted to achieve in your lifetime. I thought okay whatever, but I did it and funny thing was…most of those goals were achieved in the first 10 years.

I honestly had no idea how I would accomplishment some of those goals. Yet I did. And yet, some people have a clear vision of how they will accomplishment their goals.

Meet my friend Chris Bolger who just recently broke a Guinness Book of World Record. Not just broke it…he destroyed it.

His goal now is to smash 3 more.

Will he do it?

I believe so.

What's ironic is that Chris didn't write down his goal, nor did he want to wait 2 years, 5 years, 10 years or even his lifetime to do it.

He destroyed the Guinness Record goal just a few weeks after thinking of doing it. WOW!

Unlike my goals where I wrote down what I wanted to accomplish over the long term Chris takes goal destroying to a whole new level.

Chris suggests making your goals big and bold. Use "outside the box" thinking coupled with a work hard, play hard attitude.

It's up to you slow or fast…make your goals worth destroying.

LESSON #89

Confidence Isn't Walking Into The Room With Your Nose In The Air, And Thinking You Are Better Than Everyone Else, It's Walking Into The Room And Not Having To Compare Yourself To Anyone Else In The First Place.

Hah, you don't compare yourself to others do you?

Well, maybe you like to tell people you don't. I think on some level we all compare ourselves to somebody. It's human nature.

Why compare yourself to others?

The only one you really need to compare yourself to is you. Yep, yourself. I mean seriously, why would you compare yourself to someone who has never experienced all the things you have in life?

And if walking into a room with your nose in the air thinking you are better than everyone is confidence...think again. It's more like cockiness. And, frankly cockiness is not a trait people respect.

I know, I used to be that cocky guy who thought I was better than everyone. Ugh, the only thing cockiness gets you is less friends.

Instead of thinking you are better than everyone else, think how you can better yourself, not by comparing, but by observing.

You can learn a lot when you aren't trying to impress or judge someone.

Have confidence in yourself...it's the only way to live.

LESSON #90

Live In Such A Way That If Someone Speaks Badly Of You, No One Would Believe It.

Are we talking about the same person? Hah, I don't believe that. He wouldn't do such a thing. What? No, she isn't like that either.

There will always be people who feel the need to open their mouths and criticize without ever knowing the "real" person they are speaking ill against. Or, they feel upset that the person couldn't be swayed by their mind control games so they go off and bad mouth them to others.

Your integrity, your character, your authenticity and your moral compass is what people see, hear, feel in their hearts and know in their soul what a good person you are. And when someone speaks badly of you, no one believes it.

That's a good super power to have. Especially, in today's socially connected world.

When you offer your authentic self to others and they see the type of person you are, they know deep down you are a person of credibility and honesty, and it's like having a shield protect you from all the jealous haters.

Imagine, people you don't really know defending you from the negativity of others.

Powerful...very powerful.

Do you live your life in such a way?

If not, let's get you started… it begins by you being polite to others, being authentic, having integrity and being a friend to all.

LESSON #91

Be A Wolf. Be A Lion. Set Goals. Smash Them. Be Stronger. Be Better. Show People Who You Are. Never Apologize For Being Awesome. Stay Positive. Stay The Course.

Yep, have a "go get 'em" attitude!

Show conviction and determination. Show people what you're made of. Just be awesome.

You know it's a lot easier to read it in a book then try to be that person...I get it. Hey, I've read a lot a books too. I know where you're coming from. The "rah-rah" talks are not always motivational or you're just not in the mood to listen to them.

Been there, done that!

First, never apologize for being awesome...that's something you earned. Second, you have to stay positive...you have goals to smash...let's see you do it. And third...in to stay the course, you have to be stronger, you to be better and you have to show the world who you are.

That's it.

What are you waiting for?

Put the book down for at least 15 minutes and focus on you. Seriously. What goals can you smash this week? What distractions are preventing you from staying the course?

Figure 'em out!

You have what it takes...never give up, never surrender!

LESSON #92

Forgive Yourself.
It's One Of The Toughest Things To Do In Life, But So Important. Let Go Of The Past, You Can't Change It.
Change Yourself And
Do Great Things In The Future.

We hold ourselves victim to what we did in the past whether to ourselves or to others. Some have taken on a personal quest to right their wrongs. And, as noble as that is, it's not always the answer. In order to fix your past mistakes you are constantly reminding yourself of what you did and that just piles on more stress and frustration.

So, forgive yourself first. What you did in the past, can stay there. It has no business being dragged back up and regurgitated only to upset you and others. And frankly, what good will come of it?

We see news reporters always dragging up old dirt, pulling the proverbial skeletons out of the closet. Then, those people instead of accepting what they did and move on with it, they spend countless hours covering it up, spinning it and worrying about who knows what version of what story. Way too confusing for me.

Hey, stuff happened.

It happens to everyone. It will continue to happen. You are not the only one. That's life. Accept your past, forgive yourself then concentrate on a brighter future.

The future awaits!

Go off and do great things.

LESSON #93

Believe Deep Down In Your Heart That You Are Destined To Do Great Things. - Joe Paterno

I remember in grade school we had to take these job assessments where it would tell you, based on your answers, what job you would have when you grew up.

All the answers that were given to all the kids that day all dealt with working for someone else. It was if "the powers that be" didn't want kids to know they could be their own boss, or be an artist, a writer, a thinker, a doer or a leader.

But even as a kid I knew deep down in my heart I was destined to do great things and I wasn't going to let some stupid assessment tell me otherwise. I laughed at what the paper said I would be...and then I tore it up. It was the first time I was happy to take a detention.

If you believe you are destined for greatness don't allow others to convince you otherwise. They may say they have only the best intentions for you but what it really does is restrict how you think of yourself and your potential.

You have the ability to be and do anything you want in this great big world...why settle for what others have in store for you?

Think big!

Think bold!

Whatever it is you believe you are capable of becoming hold on to it and never let it go!

It's your destiny...and it's calling out for you!

LESSON #94

Be Brave. Take Risks.
Nothing Can Substitute Experience.
Experiment. Fail. Repeat.

I've experienced more from life, business and relationships by taking risks, from failing, and from experimenting than I ever would have if I wasn't brave.

Yep, brave!

Being brave is saying, "heck with the risks, I'm doing it anyway...and if I fail, I'll learn to do it better".

Oh, but you're worried about the failing part, right?

If you're worried, then you'd better curl up in the fetal position and go hide in a closet, now. You just failed again.

You can't hide from failure.

But you can accept it. You can even welcome it with open arms. Failing is learning what doesn't work.

When you experiment, fail and repeat you are learning. Sadly, they don't teach you how to be brave in elementary school, and they discourage children from taking risks or telling the pupils they failed. And yet, if more kids would learn this valuable lesson early on...society would be filled with some really smart, talented people.

But it's never to late to be brave and it's never wrong to take risks and fail...nothing can substitute experience...nothing!

Don't worry about failing...that's the beauty of it...you still learn.

Now be brave, take risks, experiment and fail often.

LESSON #95

If It Doesn't Challenge You, It Doesn't Change You.

You feel overwhelmed...maybe even it petrified...you've never done something like this before, you keep asking yourself why you signed up for this. And, yet you find the will to not only overcome the challenge, but find that it's somehow made you stronger.

It changed you.

You aren't afraid of that challenge anymore.

Isn't life funny that way.

The very thing that challenges you, is what changes you.

And yet, for many, the challenge is so mind numbing, so nerve racking, so brain thumping that the very thought causes them to panic, to scream, to get angry and to be mean to those around them.

They can't comprehend that the challenge ahead of them will help change them into a better person. They are blinded by what the challenge is and not how it could benefit them.

What was a challenge you had to overcome?

How did it change you?

How did you react when presented with that challenge?

Every person's concept of a challenge is different. To some it's heart attack ready to happen event to others it's just a mild speed bump on the road of life.

The more challenges you overcome...the more life changes you!

LESSON #96

We All Have Unsuspected Reserve Of Strength Inside That Emerges When Life Puts Us To The Test. -Isabel Allende

Hulk smash! Okay, maybe not that kind of strength. But it could be compared to that.

You might not turn into a giant green rage monster but, you do have unsuspected reserve of strength that emerges when life puts you to the test.

The strength I'm referring to is the ability to stand up and say, "Is that all you got, come on...heap it on me, I can take it!"

But strength isn't always about the physical.

Your mental and spiritual toughness are sometimes stronger than your actual physical strength.

My friend Owen battled cancer and won. Even when his body felt physically beaten by the chemotherapy and radiation it was his mental toughness and spiritual beliefs that pushed him to continue to fight. Life put Owen and his family through the ultimate test!

You have that unsuspected reserve of strength too.

Maybe you've experienced it. Maybe you've fought like Owen and battled life. Or maybe you just stayed calm when everyone else was panicking in a crisis. Hey, that's strength too.

You have it in you...you can control it.

You're stronger than you think.

MASTERY

The student becomes the teacher!

LESSON #97

I Will Never Quit. I Will Persevere And Thrive On Adversity, If Knocked Down I Will Get Back Up Every Time. -US Navy Seals

Remember Lesson #73?

The one about "God didn't give you the strength to get back on your feet so that you can run back to the same thing that knocked you down"?

You have two choices; walk away or fight. If life knocks you down, you get up and face the challenge head on...or figure out how to remove yourself so you don't fall victim to the adversity the next time. The choice is yours.

What would a SEAL do?

If you answered, "Never Quit!" then kudos to you. You have an attitude of a warrior. You thrive on adversity. If knocked down you get back up every time.

But a warrior also knows his/her limits. Sometimes life will challenge you to the breaking point...do you have what it takes to keep fighting?

Just because you walk away, doesn't mean you are quitting. It means you have the strength to know whats worth fighting for.

Getting knocked down gets old really quickly. Do you have the mental aptitude to keep getting back up? Running back to the very same thing that knocked you down is foolhardy but sometimes you need to fight back to show life you're not afraid.

Sometimes you need to make a stand and be a warrior!

LESSON #98

Excellence Is The Unlimited Ability To Improve The Quality Of What You Have To Offer. - Rick Pitino

Everyone has an ability. Everyone has something they are good at. But to have excellence is to have the unlimited ability to improve the quality of what you have to offer.

Think about that for a second... "unlimited ability to improve the quality of what you're offering"...wow!

Powerful!

That means you are constantly tweaking, adjusting, fixing and making better your product, service, delivery, training, communication, whatever it is...you understand the power excellence has and will stop at nothing to keep making improvements.

What do you have to offer?

How can others benefit from it?

How can you improve it?

Those questions can led to excellence in what you have to offer...but it starts with you. Do have what it takes? Excellence doesn't come easy.

In order to have an "excellence" attitude you must be willing be better in every way, shape and form. To strive for and exceed that which others are doing and give 100% percent of yourself always.

Strive for excellence! I believe in you.

LESSON #99

Thought Is Your Greatest Power To Direct And Control Your Life. - Lee Milteer

What are your thoughts right at this moment? Are they positive or negative? Do they build you up or restrict you in some way?

Did you know what you think about is what you focus on? It is! And, it's that very thing that directs and controls your life. Yep, it's the greatest power you have. Yeah, thought!

When you think negatively about something, that negativity affects you and can prevent you from achieving what you want out of life.

Your thoughts can move mountains, they can build monuments and they can create empires. They can also be the destroyer of dreams...yours!

Imagine, your thoughts have the power to change history. That's right! That history is all about you. So why continue to allow those negative thoughts to rule over you and prevent you from achieving success?

It's time you focused on you. It's time to allow positivity into your thoughts. The time for creating your empire is now. You have the power and it's all in your thoughts.

Remember Walt Disney? He thought it...then made it happen. Why can't you?

Take control of your life and direct to where you want to go.

It all starts with a thought.

What's yours?

LESSON #100

Obstacles Can't Stop You.
Problems Can't Stop You.
People Can't Stop You.
Only You Can Stop You.

That's right...only you have the power to stop you.

Throughout this book, I've showed you ways on how to improve. Were you paying attention? I certainly hope so.

There are no obstacles that can stand in your way. There are no problems you can't overcome. And there are no people that you can't face.

None! Zero! Zilch! Nada!

And if you think so...it's all in your head.

Yes, you not being able to accomplish something it's all mindset. Fear maybe? Procrastination? The thought of failing? Being humiliated? Whatever your reason...whatever your excuse...it's all you.

Nobody else can accept the blame for you not doing something. You can't blame others when you try to avoid obstacles, skirt around the problems or don't listen to people trying to help you. That my friend is all you.

So if you want to be invincible, unstoppable and able to leap over obstacles and problems with ease then you need to get out of your own way. Yep, stop bullshitting yourself and just go do it.

Quit stopping yourself and go live life to the fullest.

LESSON #101

Never Put Passion In Front Of Principle, Even If You Win You Lose. - Mr. Miyagi

Passion is the fuel that fires our desire to create a business, help a charity, continuing learning or to simply be in love with another person. The more passionate we are the more people want to be a part of what we do.

But without a moral compass to help keep us straight, our passions can lead us astray. Having principles is like having Jiminy Cricket on your shoulder telling you "Let Your Conscious Be Your Guide". Unfortunately, some people's conscious allows them to do anything they want.

Look at the American political scene, these men and women have a passion for politics, improving social economic conditions and helping reshape a country. Kudos to them, right! But, how many in your memory have been accused of violating ethics, lying to the public or falsifying records to improve their own status?

Your principles are what people admire, not your passions!

It's those principles that make you trustworthy, respected and give you credibility over those who have no principles.

If someone asks you to do something that violates your principles you need to stand your ground no matter the outcome.

Taking a stand because of your principles is never wrong. You might be tempted to put passion first and the outcome might sound awesome…but it seldom is.

Be a person of principle…and win every time!

ALMOST THE END

I would like to thank you for allowing me the opportunity to show you how to improve your life, business and relationships using *"Lessons From The Dojo"* as your guide.

Please share this book with your friends, family, colleges, your boss and whoever might benefit from it.

I would also like to ask you a favor...

If you liked this book would you take a picture with it and share it to your Facebook, Twitter or Instagram using the hashtag... **#LessonsFromTheDojo**

If reading the digital version take a picture holding your tablet, phone or Kindle device with the "Lessons From The Dojo" cover photo displaying

Oh, and please leave a 5 star review on Amazon and Barnes & Noble. This lets others know what you think and helps them decide if this book is worth the read.

www.amazon.com

www.bn.com

ABOUT THE AUTHOR

 **Rob Anspach** a former carpet cleaner turned Global Social Media Strategist, SEO Expert, Author and Speaker. Rob took the experiences learned owning a cleaning company over 20 years to first establish himself as a teacher to cleaners then an authority to entrepreneurs and corporations worldwide. Rob has also authored two social media books, *"Social Media Debunked"* and *"Share: 27 Ways to Boost Your Social Media Experience, Build Trust and Attract Followers"* and coauthored along with Paul Douglas the SEO book, *"Optimize This: How Two Carpet Cleaners Consistently Beat Web Designers On The Search Engines"*.

To learn more and connect with Rob visit
www.AnspachMedia.com

BONUS LINKS

Remember back in Lesson #45 where Rob mentions the interview he did with Steve Sims?

http://anspachmedia.com/from-bricklayer-to-high-end-concierge/

Listen as Rob Anspach is interviewed on the Rhino Daily Podcast

http://anspachmedia.com/rob-anspach-is-interviewed-on-the-rhino-daily-podcast/

RESOURCES

Blublocker Sunglasses - www.BluBlocker.com

Dr. Guillermo Alvarez - www.Endobariatric.com

Dr. Lillian Glass - www.DrLillianGlass.com

Steve Sims - www.TheBlueFish.com

Elizabeth McCormick - www.YourInspirationalSpeaker.com

Chris Bolger - www.ChrisBolgerPerformance.com

WANT TO CONTINUE YOUR LESSONS?

Join The Business Dojo!

It's a fun group page on Facebook where you can interact with other like-minded entrepreneurs and business savvy individuals.

Teaching the Art & Discipline of being a better entrepreneur.

www.facebook.com/groups/thebusinessdojo

OTHER BOOKS BY ROB ANSPACH

Optimize This: How Two Carpet Cleaners Consistently Beat Web Designers On The Search Engines - in Print or Kindle

Share: 27 Ways To Boost Your Social Media Experience, Build Trust And Attract Followers - in Print or Kindle

Social Media Debunked - Kindle Only

Books available through Amazon at

www.amazon.com/author/robertanspach

Or get autographed copies by ordering from
www.AnspachMedia.com

SHARE THIS BOOK!

I mean it!

Tell your friends all about this book.

Share where you bought it.

Share it at lunch!

Share it at the gym!

Share it on the beach!

Share it on social media.

Share it using this hashtag...

#LessonsFromTheDojo

Made in the USA
Middletown, DE
19 December 2020

26930397R00070